Dear Megan,
I hope you
gain value from
the MBP book.
Warm regards,
Christopher

CW01073000

La Petite Fleur
Publishing

Mindfulness Burnout Prevention

An 8-Week Course for Professionals

Mindfulness Burnout Prevention

An 8-Week Course for Professionals

Christopher Dines

Author of *Mindfulness Meditation: Bringing Mindfulness into Everyday Life*

MINDFULNESS
BURNOUT PREVENTION

Mindfulness Burnout Prevention: An 8-Week Course for Professionals
La Petite Fleur Publishing
Copyright © 2015 Christopher Dines
Edited by Mary McGahan
Proofread by Lizzie Ferrar
Cover design by Laura Gordon

La Petite Fleur Publishing is a small independent group of people based in England who are dedicated to releasing the highest quality books for you to enjoy. We are passionate about providing excellent spiritual/personal development fiction and non-fiction books that can contribute to global wellbeing and world peace.

La Petite Fleur Publishing uses smooth recyclable paper to help the environment and ensure a quality reading experience. We also provide digital versions of all of our titles.

Contact us by email at enquiries@lapetitefleurpublishing.com or visit us directly at www.lapetitefleurpublishing.com

Printed in the United Kingdom

ISBN: 978-0-9575631-8-6

**Other titles by Christopher Dines at La Petite Fleur
Publishing**

Mindfulness Meditation: Bringing Mindfulness into Everyday Life

Manifest Your Bliss: A Spiritual Guide to Inner Peace

The Mystery of Belief: How to Manifest Your Dreams

A Ticket to Prosperity: Spiritual Lessons for an Abundant Life

Table of Contents

Week 2: Communicating Mindfully 70

Week 3: Focus, Alertness and Concentration 86

Week 4: Mindfulness and Emotional Intelligence 102

Week 5: Emotional Resilience   131

Week 6: Body Scan Awareness and Meditation Practices 150

Week 7: Self-Compassion   162

Week 8: Cultivating Gratitude and Appreciation in the Workplace   177

Preface

Preface
Growing Concerns in the Workplace

"The greatest wealth is health."

— Virgil

A growing concern in today's workplace is that so many people are suffering from tremendous stress, burnout, depression and anxiety. This means that human performance is not being maximised and skills are not being fully utilised.

It is becoming increasingly important in today's unforgiving economic climate for employees to be able to demonstrate equanimity under pressure and for employers to take a much more serious approach to the mental health and emotional wellbeing of their staff.

Employers are under great pressure and if they are not able to remain calm and serene in today's unforgiving economic climate, their energy and demeanour will have a detrimental effect on their employees, creating an uncomfortable working environment.

The added pressures of over-time, staff shortages, deadlines, the fear of being made redundant and poor management create subconscious fears in many employees. The fears of businesses going bust or losing talented employees to competitors add to the daily stress load of even the most competent employer.

The number of offices I have walked into that carry a heavy feeling of anxiety, frustration and dullness is quite a concern. I recall being called in to a sales office in Canary Wharf, London, to help members of staff to reduce their stress levels.

The looks of frustration and the expressions of disconsolate people consumed by stress were quite alarming. To the credit of the owners of the company, they were acutely aware of this problem.

On average, most of their salesmen and women lasted nine months before moving on to another job. The pressure was taking its toll. However, after a course of mindfulness meditation and visualisation techniques their performance improved dramatically. Many other companies I have assisted in this area have seen a similar improvement in the general wellbeing of their employees.

The reality is that not everyone is fortunate enough to be working in a job that they feel deeply passionate about. This fact, compounded with the day-to-day grind that eats away at many in the workforce, means that pathological stress and emotional suffering follow. Stress, burnout and strain on the human heart are all increasingly taking their toll for millions of hardworking people. However, even someone who is working in a job that simply 'pays the bills' can turn mundane and stressful tasks into pleasant activities with a slight adjustment in attitude and by adopting a daily mindful practice.

It is therefore crucial for both employers and employees to learn to be calm, mindful and emotionally resilient in the workplace.

In a fascinating article published by HSE (Health & Safety Executive), United Kingdom, it was reported that the total number of stress-related absences in 2011/2012 was 428,000 out of 1,073,000 for all work-related illnesses. According to HSE, the pressures of today's grind are having a progressively detrimental effect on the mental and physical health of the population.

Since many of us spend most of our productive years in the workplace, the ability to transcend stress, anxiety and pressure is of paramount importance. Thankfully, more businesses are starting to see the intelligence behind honouring the mental and emotional wellbeing of their staff.

The UK National Institute for Health and Clinical Excellence has endorsed mindfulness as a wonderful practice that can be used to address depression, anxiety and stress. Likewise, the UK National Health Service has recommended mindfulness as a serious practice for mental and emotional health for over a decade.

What is alarming, however, is that, according to the BBC, the NHS revealed that there were 41,112 staff absences due to anxiety, stress, depression and burnout in 2014. This figure has almost doubled since 2010, when 20,207 employees took time off work to regain their mental and emotional wellbeing.

While assisting professionals, non-profits and companies to develop composure, calmness, emotional resilience and mindfulness in the workplace, I have observed how a few simple adjustments in daily habits can improve attitudes and performance. A negative and cluttered frame of mind can be transformed through a daily adjustment in habits and emotional resilience can be learnt.

This is why I have written this book and created the eight-week Mindfulness Burnout Prevention course for professionals. The workplace has the potential to be an open system for great work, creativity and mastery of services and products, if the individual and collective attitudes are properly geared to meet day-to-day issues as well as bigger evolutionary challenges.

All that is required from an employer or employee to gain value from this book is to have an open mind. As Herbert Spencer said, "There is a principle which is a bar against all information, which is proof against all arguments and which cannot fail to keep a man in everlasting ignorance—that principle is contempt prior to investigation".

Foreword

Foreword
Dr Barbara Mariposa

Christopher Dines is a courageous man. He is diving right into the heart of the silent epidemic of the 21st Century: burnout. He has written a book that faces the problem head on, while most people who are being affected by it are trying to ignore it. So, he is both identifying and naming the problem, bringing it out into the open and providing solutions.

When the Ebola epidemic took hold in Sierra Leone and it became apparent that First World countries were at risk, the world suddenly sat up and listened. Here was a readily identifiable, potentially life-threatening disease with a circumscribed cause, a clear clinical path of illness, and visible effects: a physical illness with a physical cause. And hopefully a cure.

In the second decade of the 21st Century, we are, in our so-called civilised societies, in the grip of an equally serious but silent and invisible epidemic: mental illness. Stress, anxiety and depression are predicted by the World Health Organization to be the second biggest cause of ill health in First World countries by 2020. Why are we not jumping up and down and throwing resources at this epidemic too?

Could it be because of the stigma associated with the word 'mental'? In this day and age, it strikes me as inexplicably uncivilised that we still fear talking about inner suffering. We can't touch it, measure it, explain it, or fix it in the same way we can a broken leg. Yet it is as real, as tangible and as crippling. It is all the more so because we're not supposed to have it. Shame, guilt, secrecy, stigma and prejudice prevail, which means that huge numbers of people are suffering in silence.

Burnout goes hand in hand with stress. Depression, anxiety, panic attacks, addictive behaviours, aggression and even violence are just some of the common outcomes. Which of these do you feel comfortable talking about? Do you know someone who has been or is affected by any of these? Would you comfortably talk about it on the bus, in the pub, at work? Probably not!

Even in the 21st Century, mental illness remains hidden. Not surprising perhaps, when a recent survey revealed that 94% of a sample of senior executives admitted to being prejudiced against people who have experienced a mental health problem; 70% of employers said they felt unable to speak about it.

This state of denial, secrecy and stigma is, in itself, part of the problem. If we were able to talk openly about our addictions, exhaustion, diminished sex drive, insomnia, and fear of failure, we would at the same time be relieving the problem. That's the paradox. And that's why I say Christopher Dines is a courageous man. He is, by writing this book, demanding that we sit up and pay attention.

Burnout is real. It's happening in an office near you. Levels of mental ill health are sky high among the skyscrapers of London. We have to get to grips with this epidemic and put both curative and preventative measures in place.

As a hardworking doctor with two small children, an alcoholic husband who got violent when drunk, and a mother with dementia living with me, I know all about burnout. I was the strong one, the one who could cope with everything. I had to. I didn't know it was okay to ask for help. Truth be told, I didn't know how to ask for help. I crashed and burned spectacularly.

I don't want this to happen to you. The work I do now is based on how I road-tested myself on the journey to full health and what I learnt along the way. I am dedicated to spreading understanding of the things that work to alleviate and prevent burnout. Beyond that, I am committed to helping you fulfil your true potential. Developing mindful self-awareness, improving emotional intelligence and cultivating compassion are at the top of the list, which is why I'm delighted to be invited to write the foreword for this book.

What causes burnout? Let's look at one of the underlying mechanisms for a moment.

Evolution moves, to paraphrase Meryl Streep's character in *The Devil Wears Prada*, at a glacial pace. The passing of 150,000 years is like the blink of an eye in evolutionary terms. 150,000 years ago (forgive the gross oversimplification), humans spent most of their time either out on the savannah focusing on the horizon, patiently waiting for prey to appear, and using great skill, presence and immaculate timing to capture and kill it, or back home round the campfire, taking care of their children, engaged in social bonding activities and tending to and gathering their crops.

How the human being is designed and functions has changed very little since then. Our brains are still wired the same way to maximise our ability to act in socially integrative ways and react strongly to external threats from outside the group, be it another tribe or a hairy mammoth.

In particular, two small almond-shaped parts of the brain, one on each side, the amygdalae, are constantly on the lookout to detect any kind of threat to our survival. When a twig cracks nearby or a branch flicks behind us, the amygdala (let's use the singular noun) sends red alert messages through the brain and body to prepare us to fight whatever is currently threatening us, or to run away from the source of danger as fast as possible.

This fight or flight response is fuelled by adrenaline and cortisol, two hormones produced by the adrenal glands which sit on top of the kidneys. These chemicals exert the following effects on the brain and body: increased heart rate, raised blood pressure, shallow breathing, digestive system shut-down, immune system shut-down, raised blood sugar, disturbance of sex hormone production, narrowing of perception, tunnel vision, inhibition of creative thinking, and a focus on self-preservation.

The same mechanism kicks in today when we feel under threat or that our survival is at stake, and when certain thought patterns kick in around self-criticism, perfectionism, or anxiety about the future. (Will I be made redundant? Will I make that deadline? Will I mess up in that meeting?)

The same mechanism kicks in because of the nature of most of the thoughts we are thinking and the unexpressed or unrecognised feelings we are experiencing.

The same mechanism kicks in simply because of the pace of life today. We were not designed to live surrounded by concrete, crammed daily into confined spaces, working in close proximity to potentially hostile co-workers, staring at computer screens for long periods of time, or sitting still for longer than an hour.

Thirty years ago, I went to the bank on a Friday lunchtime, stood in a queue for an hour or so, and paid in the business cheques. While waiting, there was no smart phone to email, message, Google, Instagram or Snapchat. I stood quietly and waited patiently, maybe chatting to someone in the queue or just noticing what was going on around me. Yesterday, I noticed that I had feelings of impatience arising when an online money transfer was taking longer than 10 seconds.

The pace of life, the way we live, the lack of space, the constant need to achieve, push, do better, compete, work long hours, and go to the gym mean we are constantly under pressure. As a result, that little part of the brain designed to detect threat is on overdrive. We feel under threat most of the time, whether we consciously know it or not.

The chemical changes in our bodies described above become not just one off and beneficial occurrences to get us out of a sticky situation, but chronic and persistent sources of ill health (physical, emotional and mental).

The human being cannot sustain this kind of pressure. The long-term result? Burnout.

It's not our fault if we get stressed, anxious, depressed, exhausted, ill, sleep badly. Or develop digestive disorders, diabetes, heart problems, breathing difficulties, loss of libido, infertility, high blood pressure. And attempt to hide our pain and suffering with addictive behaviours, denial and self-blame.

We tend to think there is something wrong with us as individuals, that we can't keep up, when in truth most other people are feeling the same. Our very biology is trying to protect us but the mechanism has been hijacked to keep us pumped up, revved up and always ready to run.

It's not your fault. But... or should I say... and...

There is a lot you can do to help yourself.

That's where the contents of this invaluable book come in.

With great gentleness and compassion, Christopher's style of writing brings you to a more peaceful place. He is inviting you to step back and take a look, take time out to re-appraise how you live your life and how you view yourself.

What habits or ways of being can smooth the path of your day-to-day life? What attitudes and approaches can allow us to work better together, with greater understanding, empathy and consideration? What can you do, right now, to cultivate skills that will help you deal better with the pressures of daily life?

How can you learn to be kinder to yourself, be your own best friend and reduce the risk of self-damage and self-harm? How will this affect the way you see yourself, your work situation, the people around you?

If you start to take care of your inner world and what happens in your thoughts and feelings, how could this improve your relationships at work, at home and with yourself?

In this book, Christopher is giving you a roadmap to sanity, health and fulfilment. By following the well-laid-out plan and taking the simple steps he suggests for you, your life will start to turn around. It takes courage to admit that you need help. Yet, the cost of not doing so is extremely high. If you keep on doing what you're doing, the way you're doing it, you'll end up where you're currently heading. If even a small part of you knows that the way you are living your life right now doesn't fulfil, nurture or do you any good, stop now. Take time out to re-appraise, be honest and be kind to yourself.

Overwork kills. And it cost an estimated £26 billion in the UK in 2012. On the basis of this alone, companies need to sit up and listen. There are huge financial implications for businesses to investing, or in most companies, not investing, in the long-term wellbeing of their staff. It makes pure business sense to give all staff the tools and techniques to develop and sustain mental and emotional wellbeing. Such tools can be found in this book.

Burnout can be prevented. It's imperative that we address this silent and invisible epidemic. 42% of workers in the financial sector have trouble relaxing. 60% admit to poor sleep. 38% of sick leave nationally is due to mental illness. Accurate figures on levels of addiction to alcohol and cocaine are difficult to obtain for obvious reasons. But just look around you. 78% of suicides in the young adult age group are male.

This last statistic is particularly sad, as it points to the current unacceptability of men asking for help. Rather than admit they are suffering, better to carry on to the point where things are so bad that there is only one way out. I know this pattern. I was there myself. I burnt out to the degree that suicide seemed like the only logical option. And believe me, when you get to that place inside yourself, it does seem like the only logical option.

In my one-to-one work and the courses I run, I am, on a daily basis, helping and listening to the stories of the high-flying professionals, architects, lawyers, CFOs, teachers and CEOs who are brave enough to seek assistance. The pressures and strains under which they are living their lives are astounding. All are driven to want to contribute, make a difference and do their best work; all are paying the price in terms of their physical, mental and emotional health. The knock-on effects that impact relationships, family and social life can be devastating.

It doesn't have to be this way. Each person has within them huge resources to change, grow and heal. To learn ways of fulfilling themselves, making that contribution and being well. The two are not mutually exclusive. Far from it. It's just a question of learning certain skills.

These skills are to be found in this book. Take your time. Allow the process to unfold. Trust that the steps you are being asked to take will have a profound and lasting impact. You may meet resistance within yourself. Change can feel uncomfortable. Include these feelings instead of excluding yourself from the opportunity to transform your life. Be patient and persevere. Encourage others to join you. Insist that courses such as this become a mandatory part of business and personal development training.

It makes perfect sense, once we open our eyes.

Dr Barbara Mariposa,
Medical Doctor and Wellness Pioneer

Introduction

Introduction
What can you expect from this book?

"I'm a great believer that any tool that enhances communication has profound effects in terms of how people can learn from each other, and how they can achieve the kind of freedoms that they're interested in."

— Bill Gates

Why should you read this book and proceed with the course, and what will you gain? After all, you have a busy life with all manner of challenges and important duties to address and attend to.

Firstly, it might be helpful to consider the following: what if, looking back over a long professional career and reflecting on your experiences, you realised that large chunks of your professional life or charitable philanthropic work had been squandered due to a lack of presence and calmness of demeanour?

What if you came to realise that your worries and anxieties about circumstances or ill-feeling towards co-workers and clients had robbed you of mental and emotional space, which could have been channelled into making you more effective, efficient, serene, creative and resilient? Surely, that would have to be considered a sad realisation, especially when there is another approach to handling the pressures of work life in the 21st Century? This is why this book can interest you and be of great value by helping you to avoid stifling your talents, skills and human potential and to prevent burnout.

Too many of us are under enormous pressure in our day-to-day life, especially in the workplace.

The stress in family, social and professional life can take its toll if we lack the ability to be calm and emotionally resilient.

Whether someone is a CEO of a major corporation or is serving meals in a diner, failure to adopt a mindful approach will mean that mental and emotional exhaustion could become a habitual condition. Whether someone is stressed about their stocks losing value or being able to pay their bills, the internal underlying conditions of stress and pressure are essentially the same.

Regardless of material environments, all human beings are subject to stress and anxiety. It is human nature to look at another person's life and believe that they 'have it better than me'. However, the reality is that it is our awareness and capacity to be calm which ultimately determines the quality of our professional, social and personal lives.

Some of us spend more time with work colleagues than with our partners, spouses, children, grandchildren and friends. Since many of us spend an average of 45 hours a week with our work colleagues, it is essential to know how to communicate in a way that is clear, calm and compassionate; otherwise a vast area of our lives will be disturbed by conflict and negativity.

For many of us, our work is a way to express our talents, apply our skills and make our contribution to society. Regardless of how our skills manifest, being of service in a business or non-profit can be a rewarding and enjoyable process.

However, if this opportunity to be of maximum service to society is undermined by anxiety and resentment, we are clearly missing the mark in amplifying human brilliance. Working diligently and being effective is much easier once we learn how to master being mindful.

The incredible benefits of practising and applying mindfulness and self-compassion in the workplace are being increasingly recognised by human resource professionals as well as the medical profession, as the stresses of competing in today's global economy take their toll on the mental health and emotional wellbeing of many otherwise talented and enthusiastic individuals in the workplace.

Learning to practise mindfulness greatly enhances our ability to manifest emotional intelligence and equanimity under pressure and to display calmness, empathy and adaptability when communicating with others, whether it be with co-workers, clients or the board of directors. Learning to apply mindfulness on a daily basis will significantly encourage a positive, creative and enthusiastic attitude at all levels in companies large and small.

If employers and employees find that, more often than not, they are happy and feel as though they are contributing to something bigger than themselves, levels of productivity and energy will reflect this.

The number of people who bounce in and out of different jobs is increasing and, when pressed for an answer, many say they leave jobs due to unhappiness, a feeling of neglect or having had mental and emotional breakdowns.

Happiness, calm and joy can be realised at work—even in working environments that appear to be mundane. Happiness, like having a clear and calm mind, is something that operates within us rather than outside of us. We can develop the habit of a cheerful spirit at work, but it does take some willingness on our part to make the necessary inner alterations in our minds and consciousness.

In this book there are many suggestions which, if integrated into your daily routine, will bring about tremendous positive change.

The process of applying Mindfulness Burnout Prevention (MBP) in the workplace or any environment has a much more far-reaching effect than simply accessing equanimity throughout the vicissitudes of life. Continuous learning helps us to stay youthful, sharpen our mental faculties and wire new neural connections in our brain (making us better equipped to accomplish); it is also a sign of humility.

We have a wonderfully plastic and adaptable organ to use called the human brain, and to nourish such a phenomenal tool via the practice of mindfulness is a wonderful way to enhance our wellbeing and all-round success.

As you will come to understand further on in this course, the effects of mindfulness meditation on the human brain are staggering and will give you a greater opportunity to expand your awareness and develop enthusiasm for living in the same way that a baby enjoys exploring its new world.

If you put in the work to temper your emotional cycles and foster a resilient and friendly attitude, you will see how assimilating mindfulness into our habits is invaluable. After all, no one can hold down a demanding job or be an effective family member or friend without the capacity to remain calm, no matter how great the challenges thrown at us.

The greatest enemy in life is our lower nature and our unregulated, self-detrimental habits. This is why the comic character Pogo said, "We have seen the enemy and it is us".

8-Week Course for Professionals

Getting Started

Make a conscious choice to follow through with this course. Sign a commitment to your innermost self to put 100% effort into *Mindfulness Burnout Prevention: An 8-Week Course for Professionals.* This symbolises your intention to enhance calmness and mindfulness in the workplace.

Sign your name below and add the date:

_____

"When I collapsed in April 2007, I was—by our society's definition—
very successful, but by any sane definition of success, I was not. As
long as our culture defines success as money and power, we're stuck
on a treadmill of stress, sleep deprivation, and burnout."

– Arianna Huffington, founder of *Huffington Post* and author of
Thrive (quote from *Mindful Magazine*)

For so many of us, stress, anxiety, compulsive thinking, destructive
addictive patterns and fear gradually eat away at us, and if we neglect
to address this, emotional and physical breakdown and burnout can
result. This book helps to reduce the risk of professional burnout and
also addresses challenges such as stress and anxiety in the workplace,
making the course helpful for both addressing the immediate issues
and preventing the manifestation of even more serious outcomes. If
we can apply mindfulness practice and take care of our mental,
emotional and physical wellbeing, we will greatly reduce the chances
of burnout.

I recall burning out in a previous career in music in the early/mid
2000s and it took me six months to recover. This was due to taking

on far too much work, insufficient sleep, lacking present-moment awareness and resentments building up towards other professionals. Eventually, this took its toll.

This is why in the book, *Mindfulness Meditation: Bringing Mindfulness into Everyday Life*, I wrote: "In today's fast-paced world, it is very easy to get lost in the creative process of 'doing' and manifesting new ideas. Making new things happen is fun. After all, this world is a playground to co-create our reality with the universe. However, as expressed previously, when the sole purpose of one's life becomes lost in 'doing' rather than 'being', mental and emotional suffering will dominate one's experience".

To see people suffer from burnout is not pleasant—it affects them and their families and triggers financial insecurities. Below are bullet points stating what usually triggers burnout in the workplace:

- Work overload
- Exhaustion
- Painful and dysfunctional personal and professional relationships
- Compulsive worrying and an obsessive need to control outcomes and results
- Unwise lifestyle choices and negative influences
- Hostile working environments
- Placing earning capacity ahead of one's wellbeing
- Harbouring resentment, ill feeling and negative emotions
- A lack of mindfulness and self-compassion

Generally speaking, burnout amongst professionals can be avoided by making it a priority to take care of ourselves, just as we would care for a child. Regular downtime, self-kindness, plenty of sleep and applying the teachings in this course will be of great value.

In the 21st Century, we have more distractions than ever before. The hunger to get ahead often drives us to take on more work than we can handle. The temptation to 'do more', if not properly tempered, can lead to exhaustion. This can easily happen when success comes calling at our door, just as it can when we are in the early stages of building a career—we feel that we should capitalise on any opportunity to earn more money for fear of it not lasting.

How mindfulness helps us to rewire our brains

The human brain is incredible in its capacity to heal and rewire itself. The human brain can be shaped and trained to be more resilient, calm, compassionate and alert—we can condition ourselves to be successful. Through mindfulness meditation, we can literally re-wire our brains through new experiences, which modify our neural network and our neural chemistry. Mindfulness also enhances gamma synchrony and improves the function of the human brain.

To gain a better understanding of how mindfulness regulates our emotional reactions and responses, it is worth briefly covering the areas of the human brain which cause our emotional state.

The brainstem is where the 'fight, flight or freeze' response is located. This is the primitive area of the brain. The brainstem works together with the limbic area of the brain to generate our emotions and memories and regulate how we respond in our relationships. Thus, the brainstem and the limbic area work together.

Many of our instincts and reactions are driven by the subcortical area of the brain, including the feedback from the human body, such as our heart pumping, etc. This loop of the brainstem, the limbic area and subcortical area and the body are essentially what make up and govern our 'emotional mind'.

According to many neural scientists, our cortex developed when we became mammals and the pre-frontal cortex evolved later on. The prefrontal cortex is the most evolved part of the human brain. Thankfully, this part of the brain permits us to *respond* rather than *react* to our compulsions and impulses.

This works through fibres coming down from the prefrontal area of the brain to the limbic and brainstem area, calming irrational impulses. If this process does not manifest, we will always be unconsciously reacting to things, behaving similarly to our ancient ancestors, who were gravely emotionally undeveloped.

For example, if we are unable to be mindful and aware of our thought process and emotions when confronted by a potential danger (real or imagined), this will trigger 'fear' and the compulsion to fight, fly or freeze will be activated. When we are governed by these primitive emotions, the rational and logical part of the brain is over-ridden, triggering us to behave in irrational ways.

This is where mindfulness becomes relevant. For instance, if someone says something to you that would normally trigger a reaction of fear or anger, the prefrontal cortex part of the human brain can pause and bring clarity, calmness and alertness to transcend the reactions of the unregulated emotional side of the brain.

The prefrontal cortex regulates the other areas of the brain, not unlike a powerful jet of water extinguishing a bush-fire. Mindfulness or awareness-presence improves the function of the pre-frontal cortex in the human brain, enhancing the potential for better social behaviour, kindness, compassion and emotional intelligence.

Once the practice of mindfulness becomes habitual, this incredible process rewires our neural network to change our reality (life). As the saying goes in neural science, 'neurons that fire together, wire together'.

Seeing that the thoughts and emotions we impress on the human brain will change brain activity and our behaviour, the realisation of mindfulness works wonders in training our brains to help us realise a more desirable and successful reality.

The great value of mindfulness

Recent studies on the benefits of mindfulness carried out in institutions such as The University of Massachusetts and the

Mind/Body Medical Institute at Harvard University have yielded amazing results. Below are several bullet points that show the value of mindfulness:

- Improved cognitive function
- Improved productivity and enhanced resilience
- Improvement in overall wellbeing
- Enhanced creativity and personal initiative
- Improved relationships
- Improved learning, concentration, memory and focus
- Reduced stress
- Lower blood pressure
- Improved memory
- Enhanced immune system
- Less depression and greatly reduced anxiety and worry
- Better sleep

Mindfulness and cognitive function

The University of California, Santa Barbara, found that college students who practised mindfulness excelled in verbal reasoning and experienced improvements in their working memory.

The Association for Psychological Science (previously the American Psychological Society) wrote: "Our results suggest that cultivating mindfulness is an effective and efficient technique for improving cognitive function, with wide-reaching consequences".

Course outline

The Mindfulness Burnout Prevention 8-week course entails the following: Week 1: Present-Moment Awareness, Equanimity and Calmness – Week 2: Communicating Mindfully – Week 3: Focus, Alertness and Concentration – Week 4: Mindfulness and Emotional Intelligence – Week 5: Emotional Resilience – Week 6: Body Scan Awareness and Meditation Practices – Week 7: Self-Compassion – Week 8: Cultivating Gratitude and Appreciation in the Workplace.

Some of the exercises are to be applied outside of the workplace (home study) to enhance the 8-week course and gain maximum value. If you give 100% in your efforts towards this course, your mental and emotional well-being will improve, as will your capacity to respond to life in a calm and mindful manner. Once the practice has become habitual, it will be easier to make mindful living second nature in the workplace or in any other area of our lives.

Access MP3 guided meditations

Naturally, this course has included guided meditation MP3s for you to listen to upon awakening. To access the MP3s, email **mp3@christopherdines.com**. You will receive an automatic reply with an instant downloadable link to your guided meditation series. If you prefer to, you can always burn the MP3 onto CD—the choice is yours.

Week 1 –
Present-Moment Awareness,
Equanimity and Calmness

"I have just three things to teach: simplicity, patience, compassion.
These three are your greatest treasures."

— Lao Tzu

In Germany, 1948, a boy was born into what he described as an unhappy family environment and a climate of collective emotional heaviness after the years of general insanity surrounding the time of World War II.

His parents, like many, fought with each other until a separation manifested. Depressed, alone and often playing by himself, the young boy moved to Spain to live with his father where, rather than attending regular school, he studied at home.

After having what appeared to be a decent opportunity to have a good education while living in England studying various interesting subjects, the young man hit the depths of depression at the age of 29— suicidal thoughts overtook him, which was a gateway to the process of inner transformation. Thankfully, he did not take his life and carried on uncovering his understanding of reality and how he fitted into it. The young man walked the streets for several years, sometimes living rough on Hampstead Heath, London, before organically evolving into teaching self-awareness and meditation.

During the next few years, an unexpected desire to share his insight and write a book became apparent; his book was eventually published in 1997. It went on to become internationally appreciated as a classic in the field of meditation, making the author a new world spokesman on mindfulness and presence-awareness.

His name is Eckhart Tolle and his first book, considered to be his best work, was *The Power of Now*. Had Eckhart Tolle taken his life during his darkest moments, he would have tragically denied himself a fulfilling and prosperous life and would have not been able to assist millions of people in uncovering peace of mind and tranquillity.

On the subject of accessing the present moment (mindfulness), Eckhart Tolle wrote in his wonderful book: "As soon as you honour the present moment, all unhappiness and struggle dissolve, and life begins to flow with joy and ease. When you act out the present-moment awareness, whatever you do becomes imbued with a sense of quality, care, and love—even the most simple action".

What is mindfulness?

Mindfulness (present-moment awareness) is deliberately focusing our attention on our thoughts, emotions, feelings, sensations and mental activity without losing awareness of what is happening in the present moment. It is essentially being in a state of present-moment awareness and maintaining clarity without being swayed or distracted by mental commentary.

Although mindfulness has been around for thousands of years and came from the Eastern Wisdom Traditions, it is only in the last 10/15 years that scores of scientific papers have been published, emphasising the enormous value mindfulness has to offer.

For instance, mental and emotional wellbeing can be greatly improved and stress, burnout, anxiety, addictive thinking and depression can be alleviated by committing to mindfulness practice.

We can be mindful of our state of mind but we can also be mindful of the quality of our work (or lack of it), our communication skills, our ability to pay attention to detail and our capacity to develop qualities that lead to long-term success and fulfilment. In other words, the more awareness we have of ourselves and others, the more effective we will be in our professional lives.

What is equanimity?

Equanimity is a reflection of a mindful professional and is an essential quality to develop. Equanimity is a state of mental and emotional composure undisturbed by feelings of discomfort, pain and uncertainty or vicissitudes.

Equanimity is virtually impossible to cultivate without being mindful of our thoughts, feelings, patterns of behaviour and emotional triggers.

It helps us to enhance our emotional and social intelligence and create better relationships, whether it be with fellow workers, clients or the board of directors.

What is calmness?

Calmness is the realisation of peace of mind and tranquility in the present moment. Like equanimity, calmness flows through a mindful professional. It can be accessed in relaxed or alert states of mind and brings about an awareness and appreciation of our challenges and opportunities.

We cannot fight the human mind

We cannot control the mind by trying to force it to be peaceful or positive. Many have attempted this using a plethora of methods throughout the ages, but it simply does not work. Trying to fight the human mind is like walking into a lion's den empty-handed and believing that you have a realistic chance of defending yourself.

The only way to free ourselves from the grips of compulsive thinking is to completely transcend it. By this, I mean learning to observe our mental activity without being drawn into identifying with each and every thought.

A metaphor we can use is of walking into a building as an inspector with a visitor's badge and noticing all sorts of positive and negative aspects. We might notice that the building has a sound fire exit but that some of the windows need replacing. However, as a visitor, we do not need to be emotionally affected by what we have observed. We can simply note our observations and leave whenever we like. We can do the same with thoughts. When they start to become too hyperactive or troublesome, we can make a conscious choice to transcend them.

A simple day-to-day morning practice

How a person prepares themselves mentally and emotionally in the morning tends to set the momentum for the rest of the day. This is why a practice of calming the mind and slowing down compulsive thinking on awakening is so critical.

Generally speaking, 20 minutes really ought to be put aside to flow into mindfulness meditation before we start to participate in activities. If we meditate after a shower or breakfast, we have given compulsive thinking an opportunity to take hold, which will make our practice less effective.

If 20 minutes sounds too daunting to a beginner, then he or she can always start by putting 10 minutes aside for the first two weeks to practise mindfulness meditation. Once the 10-minute daily practice has become familiar, the time can be increased to 15 minutes for a two-week period and so on.

The intention is to reach the 20-minute mark every morning (including days off) in order to gain the incredible benefits of mindfulness meditation. Some long-term meditators will put 40 to 60 minutes aside daily, but when embarking on a regular meditation practice 20 minutes is sufficient.

Naturally, the desirable practice should bring mindfulness into everyday life; starting the day with a still mind is a great way of realising this.

Being conscious of our breathing

Conscious breathing anchors us into the nowness of life and gives us a fresh outlook, no different from how a baby observes reality without mental commentary. The baby enjoys watching the world and human activity without any limiting mental concepts spoiling his or her perception. Naturally, we all have to evolve from the helpless state of babyhood, but to be able to tap into that wonderful ability and truly BE in the moment is immensely liberating.

Conscious breathing is being aware of the life breath that flows within and through us without any effort on our behalf. When we make a conscious choice to observe the life breath, enjoying and appreciating our breathing, we tame and calm the mind.

We observe that we are all in rhythm with the breath that we require in order to function and live in our bodies. Just as we are dependent on the sun to keep our planet fruitful and plentiful and just as the sun is connected to us, we too are all connected to the collective life breath.

When we meditate and honour our breathing, we realise that the life breath does not change and is the most consistent process in our lives. Our bodies change as we move through the various chapters of the life cycle. Our opinions, beliefs, perspectives and perceptions change. Even the transmutation of our planet evolves every second. However, the life breath remains constant until we draw our last breath. This indicates that the life breath transcends the polarity and changes in life.

Learning to observe our breathing

There are numerous ways to practise conscious breathing; however, some simple techniques are listed below. First of all, let us be aware that we are breathing:

- When we inhale, give our full attention to the inhaled breath and notice how our entire body is in tune to this and is also breathing in.
- When we exhale, give our full attention to the entire life breath flowing out of us and observe how our body is in harmony with this mindful movement. This is a natural flow, which does not require anything else from us apart from an alertness and a commitment to be fully aware of the breath. It is important to remind ourselves throughout the day to notice that the life breath is enriching our mind and body and sustains humanity and all mammals on Earth.

How do we apply mindfulness meditation?

- We can either sit down on the floor in the lotus position or on a chair, preferably with our backs straight.

- When we are comfortable, close our eyes.
- Give our full attention to the natural flow of the life breath. We are always breathing, but because most of us lead busy lives we pay no attention to it. It is important not to force the life breath. Just be comfortably aware of it.
- Anytime the mind starts to wander off (reliving memories or visualising future events), bring our attention back to the life breath. Feel the stomach gently rise up and down as we breathe in and out and tune into the rhythm of our heartbeat.
- Then, let us begin to observe our thoughts and be aware of our feelings. Whether we have a positive or negative thought or a positive or negative emotion, we can simply be aware of it without resisting it. Eventually, this practice will dissolve the compulsive stream of thoughts and emotions. Stillness can then be realised.
- Practise this for at least 20 minutes in the morning and in the evening. However, it is important to bring awareness of your thoughts, emotions and the life breath into your activities throughout the day. If you are able to practise this more often, huge benefits will be felt. Remain alert and give your full attention to the present moment as often as possible.

How do we apply conscious deep breathing?

- Breathe deeply and inhale, counting for four seconds from one to four. As we inhale deeply, while counting from one to four, let us pay attention to the breath entering the body.
- Then, as we exhale deeply, count down from four to one. This can be repeated for several minutes, which is a powerful way to deepen our day-to-day breathing. We can repeat this cycle of breathing by extending the counting as our lungs and body become more receptive to inhaling and exhaling for longer

periods. For instance, at a later stage, we can train our body to inhale for 10 seconds and exhale for 10 seconds. This is particularly helpful when it comes to expelling anxious, stressed or even sluggish emotions.

A full-time mindfulness practice – an ancient story

After 10 years of mindfulness training, Tenno accomplished the honour of ranking as a Zen teacher. One day, Tenno decided to meet the famous Zen master Nan-in. When Tenno walked into the master's home, Nan-in greeted him with a question: "Did you leave your wooden clogs and umbrella on the porch?"

"Yes," swiftly replied Tenno.

Nan-in paused for a moment and, looking Tenno in the eye, responded by asking, "Tell me. Did you place your umbrella to the left of your shoes or to the right?"

The newly trained Zen teacher blushed as he did not know the answer—he realised that he was not truly being mindful in all of his activities. Later that evening, he asked the Zen master Nan-in to teach him how to be mindful for 10 more years.

Composure

If someone presents a front of 'doing okay' but is filled with seething inner rage or anxiety and fear, their actions will make others feel unsettled. By and large, employees and employers who never address their anger and pretend to be 'fine' make other co-workers feel terribly uncomfortable.

Pretending to be peaceful when we are anxious, angry and holding on to feelings of victimisation is counterproductive and will not put us in a favourable position to be of maximum service. You and I can both tell if someone is angry, even if their behaviour might indicate otherwise. The Wisdom Traditions warn us of the consequences of pretending to sow healthy seeds when we are, as a matter of fact, planting unhealthy ones: "You have sown much and harvested little".

It is always better to address feelings of anger and frustration without suppressing them or expressing them in a regrettable way.

The Victorian author James Allen realised the importance of a professional possessing the qualities of calmness and composure when he wrote, "The more tranquil a man becomes, the greater is his success, his influence, his power for good. Even the ordinary trader will find his business prosperity increase as he develops a greater self-control and equanimity, for people will always prefer to deal with a man whose demeanour is strongly equable".

The following tasks will be sufficient to amplify this course and will assist you to be more calm and present.

Calmness negates exaggeration

Calmness is a quality that allows us to temper our emotions and communicate with people in a favourable way. Calmness is perhaps one of the finest qualities that we can access. You do not need to be a trained Zen master to be calm; however, an honest desire to realise equanimity and resilience is necessary to maximise your potential in the workplace.

Calmness can be realised in relaxed or alert states of consciousness and is a reflection of mindfulness. For instance, if you are a person who gets very easily excited, loses their temper too often or is repeatedly rattled by the slightest annoyance, your perception of reality will be exaggerated.

A thought life based on distortion and exaggeration can only lead to repeated misjudgements and unwise decisions. Naturally, this is not desirable in our professional lives. An ability to feel emotionally steady in the face of perceived victory or loss, boom and bust, can be called calmness or mindfulness realised in one's consciousness.

To be calm is imperative for professionals. The fact is that there are cycles and different seasons which grant us vast abundance, average returns and, sometimes, poor results. This is the natural cycle of life.

Even the largest corporations or non-profit organisations will have seasons of financial loss or great unforeseen challenges to contend with and thus the professional who can display calmness and resilience throughout will be a huge asset.

Equanimity during vicissitudes

Whether you are in the business of selling stocks, cooking delicious food, cleaning an office, running a mental health unit, or teaching a child how to read and write, equanimity is an essential quality.

Without demonstrating equanimity and being aware of our thoughts, we are often likely to be operating from a place of anxiety, fear and ambivalence. While in these negative emotional states, irrational tendencies are bound to manifest. We are far more likely to make rash decisions or display reckless qualities if we are consumed by fear.

When we are calm and fully present in the moment, we are able to override emotional triggers and knee-jerk reactions which cause distress to ourselves and those around us.

So many of us have developed a habit of letting our emotions get the better of us by lashing out whenever circumstances are challenging, even having outbursts over trivial things. This does not make for a harmonious working environment.

Naturally, being human, we are going to experience discomforting emotions and we might occasionally say something regrettable in the heat of the moment or make rash choices. However, with a sincere desire to be mindful and develop equanimity, we can lessen the probability of letting ourselves down in the workplace (or at home, for that matter).

With respect to demonstrating equanimity, in the Eastern Wisdom Traditions it says clearly: "Perform your duty and abandon all attachment to success or failure". Saint Francis de Sales said, "Never be in a hurry; do everything quietly and in a calm spirit. Do not lose your inner peace for anything whatsoever, even if your whole world seems upset".

Likewise, the poet Rudyard Kipling wrote, "If you can meet with triumph and disaster, treat those impostors just the same". All three statements suggest that we remain calm (keep our wits) under all circumstances. Similarly, many successful employers have also cultivated an attitude of equanimity in the workplace.

Men and women who demonstrated equanimity

Having worked as a shepherd, a book-keeper and cowherd, later becoming a politician, philosopher and wisdom teacher, a humble Chinese man who lived from 551–479 BC had quite a life.

From being a father who experienced the deaths of two of his sons to relentlessly working to bring morality into government and finding great resistance to his stance on equality during his political career, the great teacher had a knack for remaining calm despite all sorts of discouraging circumstances.

His name was Confucius, and the effectiveness and wisdom he demonstrated in his professional life went on to shape the way humanity observed equality. Confucius stated that, "The gem cannot be polished without friction, nor man perfected without trials".

In Nebraska, Omaha, United States, Steve Forbes, from *Forbes Magazine*, was conducting a rare interview with a popular and globally recognised recording artist and one of the most effective financial investors of our time.

These two men were Sean Carter, known by his stage name Jay Z, and the investor Warren Buffett. The nature of this interview was to inspire viewers to stay positive and share gems of wisdom for developing a harmonious attitude and prosperity consciousness, particularly during a time of economic hardship for millions of hard-working people.

The scene was an unusual one in that it brought together a group of people who would not ordinarily socialise. Nonetheless, both of the men being interviewed emphasised the importance of remaining calm even when circumstances might suggest otherwise.

When asked about the secret to success, Warren Buffet replied: "What you do need is emotional stability. You have to be able to think independently. When you come to a conclusion you have to really not care what other people say and just follow the facts and follow your reasoning and that's tough for a lot of people".

In other words, Warren Buffet was suggesting that, when we make a sound decision (a choice that has been carefully considered), we have to remain calm and be emotionally resilient even if others are trying to sway our decision. Someone who is unaware of their emotional cycles and thought process will find this extremely difficult to do compared to the professional who is mindful and has a sound temperament.

The first published female writer in the British North American colonies, Anne Bradstreet (born 1612), had a positive outlook on human challenges and favoured equanimity. She wrote: "If we had no winter, the spring would not be so pleasant; if we did not sometimes taste of adversity, prosperity would not be so welcome".

The Emmy-award-winning comedian and actress Gilda Radner, who carved out an incredibly successful career and struggled with grave health problems, once said with respect to equanimity: "I wanted a perfect ending. Now I've learned the hard way that some poems don't rhyme, and some stories don't have a clear beginning, middle, and end. Life is about not knowing, having to change, taking the moment and making the best of it, without knowing what's going to happen next. Delicious ambiguity".

When interviewed on *The Oprah Winfrey Show* with respect to spending 27 years in prison for his stance against apartheid, the destructive racial segregation system in South Africa, Nelson Mandela joyfully answered questions with a great sense of humour, humility and openness.

When asked how he transcended the desire for revenge and how he was able to start the process of forgiveness in action while serving in the highest office in South Africa, Nelson Mandela replied: "Our emotions said the white minority is an enemy; we must never talk to them. But our brains said if you don't talk to this man, your country will go up in flames and for many years to come, this country would be engulfed with rivers of blood. So we had to reconcile that conflict and our talking to the enemy was the result of the domination of the brain over emotions".

The Austrian neurologist, psychiatrist and author of the classic book *Man's Search for Meaning*, Viktor E. Frankl, made a conscious choice to not feel like a victim even though he most certainly had good cause to wallow in self-pity. On 25th September 1942, Viktor E. Frankl, along with his wife, brother and parents, was forced into a Nazi concentration camp.

For much of that time, his skills were used to monitor the health of prisoners in the concentration camp until he was compelled into hard slave labour for five months in 1944 and came to realise that his wife, Tilly Frankl, had died at Bergen-Belsen concentration camp, his mother had been killed in a gas chamber and his brother Walter had died working in a mining operation.

These inhumane and cruel circumstances robbed him of those closest to him as well as his basic liberty and freedom. However, Viktor E. Frankl made up his mind, while going through his horrendous ordeal, to not allow himself to think like a victim. By doing so, he was able to preserve his own dignity and sanity.

He went on to say: "The one thing you can't take away from me is the way I choose to respond to what you do to me. The last of one's freedoms is to choose one's attitude in any given circumstance".

An ancient story on equanimity

A classic ancient story illustrates the importance of equanimity and emotional resilience beautifully.

Once upon a time, there was a wise old farmer who had worked on the land for over 40 years. One morning, while walking to his stable, he noticed that his horse had run away. His neighbours came to visit and sympathetically said to the farmer, "Such bad luck".

"Maybe," the farmer replied.

The following morning, however, the horse returned, bringing with it three other wild horses. "Such good luck," the neighbours exclaimed.

"Maybe," the farmer replied.

The following afternoon, his son tried to ride one of the untamed horses and was thrown off, causing him to break his leg. The neighbours came to visit and tried to show sympathy and said to the farmer, "how unfortunate".

"Maybe," answered the farmer.

The following morning military officials came to the farmer's village to draft young men into the army to fight in a new war. Observing that the farmer's son's leg was broken, they did not draft him into the war.

The neighbours congratulated him on his good luck and the farmer calmly replied, "Maybe".

The habit of mindful living

The biologist and author Richard Sheldrake once said on the subject of habit: "I would say that the bulk of nature is habitual, it works on habits. The so called laws of nature are actually more like habits. These are the regularities of nature based on memory, which becomes habitual and largely unconscious because habits, even in us, are unconscious".

Many people have become aware of the wonderful benefits that mindfulness and emotional resilience can bring into their professional life, but find that they cannot bring themselves to practise this in their private lives.

Even though they admit that they know it is good for them, many do not follow it through. Why is this? It is down to their inveterate behaviour. They might start sitting down to practise mindfulness meditation every morning and keep it up for a week or so but then slip back into their usual haphazard routine.

A successful businesswoman I was assisting in this area had attended a workshop on mindfulness meditation and wanted to develop the habit. Unfortunately, she found that she was able to practise mindfulness for a week or so but then resistance would set in and she would drop her practice.

I suggested to her that this was the point at which she ought to set aside a specific time each morning (ideally 20 minutes) and time herself so that the meditation practice became a habit. I emphasised to her that it was particularly important to apply this discipline at times when she really did not feel like it or felt that she did not have "enough time". Ironically, she was able to override her comfort zone by building a successful business but she didn't consider applying the same principle to her meditation practice.

She had to use her awareness over her emotions and feelings. Naturally, after a couple of months it became easier to apply this habit—she started to notice that it was easier to be mindful and calm throughout her day as a result of her morning practice.

Make a resolution to be calm and mindful

What people tend to forget or might not even be aware of is that they can consciously create an intention upon awakening to be calm and mindful throughout the day. Intention is extremely powerful and is what prompts us to move into action and get things done. It makes us more conscious.

For example, take a master meditator who has been practising mindfulness for decades. He/she spends most of his/her time in the present moment. He/she must, however, resolve to be present in the first place. When we speak of intention, we are not referring to a thought or an emotion. After all, most of our thoughts and emotions are repetitive and often muddle our clarity and judgement. No one actually knows where intention comes from, which is fascinating.

We know in our mindfulness practice that we can observe our thoughts and emotions without judging them, but behind this ancient practice is an 'intention' prompting us to remain in awareness. Therefore, make use of intention and let it gradually transform you into a more emotionally grounded and mindful human being.

Exercises

Task 1

Every day (including weekends) for seven days, put a minimum of 20 minutes aside in the morning to observe the natural flow of your breathing and to watch your thoughts and emotions. It is strongly suggested that you do this before you start any other morning activities, when the mind is easier to tame. *You may choose to listen to the guided meditations on the MP3 that was included with this course.*

Task 2

Pause as often as possible throughout the day and remind yourself that you are breathing. Ask questions such as, 'Am I breathing?', 'Who is the *awareness* that is aware of my breathing?' and 'Can I feel the life breath flow through me?' Even finding yourself fully present in the moment for three seconds or so, several times an hour, will help to keep your mind clear, calm and alert.

Task 3

Every evening before you retire at night, reflect and be honest with yourself. Answer the following questions to increase your mindfulness practice:

Did you discipline yourself to practise mindfulness meditation that morning for 20 minutes before embarking on your day-to-day activities? If so, how did you find your meditation? Were there any repetitive patterns of thought or emotion that persisted and were you able to observe that you are not your thoughts and feelings?

Were you able to witness your mind activity and detach from your thoughts? Did you have any moments of calm and tranquillity during any of your formal sitting meditation practices? Did you notice any subtle realisations of serenity during the day?

Day 1: Reflect and answer the questions.

Day 2: Reflect and answer the questions.

Day 3: Reflect and answer the questions.

Day 4: Reflect and answer the questions.

_____

_____

_____

_____

_____

_____

_____

_____

_____

_____

_____

_____

_____

_____

_____

_____

_____

_____

_____

_____

_____

_____

_____

_____

_____

_____

_____

_____

_____

Day 5: Reflect and answer the questions.

Day 6: Reflect and answer the questions.

Day 7: Reflect and answer the questions.

_____
_____
_____
_____
_____
_____
_____
_____
_____
_____
_____
_____
_____
_____
_____
_____
_____
_____
_____
_____
_____
_____
_____
_____
_____
_____
_____
_____
_____
_____

A Summary of Week 1

To be present and calm – what does this mean?

- Calmness is a realisation in consciousness that permits a human being to feel safe and emotionally grounded in the face of positive or negative circumstances. It is a state of being free from agitation and excitement; it carries with it a serene feeling.
- Mindfulness is an awareness of reality as it is, being fully aware of the present moment—being aware of our thoughts, emotions, habits and motives.
- Being mindful means that we can respond rather than react in a rational manner without panicking or having sudden emotional outbursts.
- To be calm and demonstrate equanimity means we are able to address a challenge with clarity, awareness and emotional intelligence rather than looking at a problem with an exaggerated perception.

Why are presence, calmness, and equanimity essential in the workplace?

- Without being calm, mindful and resilient, we cannot live to our full potential and be effective in our family life, professional life, community and society.
- Without calmness and resilience, we will be reacting to every emotion we feel and this is likely to create disharmony.

- Through mindfulness we can be in the present moment and give our undivided attention to the tasks and objectives at hand.
- We can directly improve our relationships with others by being calm and mindful of how we communicate with them.
- It will be easier to demonstrate excellent work if we are able to emotionally handle the pressures in this world and especially in the workplace by developing resilience.
- With calmness, we will be able to address stress, strain and pressure with relative ease.
- We will be less likely to succumb to depression and anxiety and other stress-related conditions.
- No one wants to spend time with someone who lacks self-control or attempts to mask their inner rage and anger.

Week 2 – Communicating Mindfully

"Communication—the human connection—is the key to personal and career success."

– Paul J. Meyer

Learning how to communicate more effectively and building healthy professional relationships in the workplace is a great asset. Whether it is a relationship with our broker, accountant, client or colleague, the quality of our relationships will ultimately determine the quality of our lives. The most effective way to build desirable professional relationships is to communicate in a calm and mindful way. Professionals who have developed the habit of creating mindful relationships, more often than not, tend to be the most effective.

Thankfully, learning to communicate with clarity is something that most of us can manage.

It pays to understand our colleagues and clients

If you seriously reflect and meditate on the value that understanding and awareness can have in your career and personal life, you will fully subscribe to the realisation that it pays to keep our emotions in check and display a compassionate attitude. As the aforementioned Eric Hoffer once said: "Compassion is the antitoxin of the soul: where there is compassion even the most poisonous impulses remain relatively harmless".

Making a conscious effort to understand and be sensitive to others' boundaries in the workplace can make all the difference. For instance, some people are naturally very tactile and express their appreciation by greeting colleagues and friends with hugs and kisses on the cheek.

Conversely, others are very reserved and feel uncomfortable with any form of physical contact other than a handshake. They might, however, prefer to give someone a genuine compliment or engage in a conversation on how the other person is doing to show their empathy.

Some of us find it easier to process new information through visual images, others through sound and feeling, and so on. By being mindful, understanding and paying attention to why our colleagues and clients behave in the way they do, it will be easier to communicate with them in a harmonious way.

Seeing ourselves in others

When you can begin to see the similarities between you and your work colleagues in respect of 'being human' and the collective challenges we all face, it makes life much easier to deal with, especially when met with overbearing behaviour. Once we can recognise our own human frailties, our assets and our undeveloped areas, it is easier to accept those of our colleagues.

Even if one has already developed suitable qualities to be a kind, decent and effective human being, the person with humility knows that this is a result of a sound habit and knows that those characteristics could easily regress to destructive behaviours without vigilance or through complacency.

Developing empathy and understanding

By and large, the human condition brings with it its share of pain and suffering. Therefore, let us refrain from punishing ourselves by being over-remorseful and worrying about the future and similarly let us be kind, understanding and empathetic towards ourselves and our fellow workers and clients. All of us hurt and we all have our different coping mechanisms.

This is why the writer James Baldwin said: "You think your pain and your heartbreak are unprecedented in the history of the world, but then you read. It was books that taught me that the things that tormented me most were the very things that connected me with all the people who were alive, or who had ever been alive".

Similarly, while giving a talk to graduates at Stanford University, the philanthropist Melinda Gates stated that: "When we consider all of our luck and privilege and where we would be without them it becomes much easier to see someone who is poor and say, 'that could be me'. And that's empathy! Empathy tears down barriers and it opens up whole new frontiers for optimism".

Empathy produces better professional relationships

With a realisation of empathy and compassion, we can use our own challenges to communicate more effectively with others. If we have, for example, ever dipped in our general performance at work, knowing what this feels like can help us to lend a supportive hand or share some helpful words with someone who is lacking in confidence or going through a challenging time. To let our hearts harden to the extent that we lose touch with our humanity is a tragedy and, thankfully, empathy, compassion and open-mindedness prevent this.

This is why Albert Einstein said: "A human being is a part of the whole called by us universe, a part limited in time and space. He experiences himself, his thoughts and feeling as something separated from the rest, a kind of optical delusion of his consciousness. This delusion is a kind of prison for us, restricting us to our personal desires and to affection for a few persons nearest to us. Our task must be to free ourselves from this prison by widening our circle of compassion to embrace all living creatures and the whole of nature in its beauty".

Naturally, an employer or employee who can display emotional intelligence and who is able to deal calmly with people from all walks of life will have a great advantage over someone who lacks empathy. If we learn to mindfully develop healthy relationships, work life becomes far more fulfilling and enjoyable. Conversely, if we do not have evolutionary relationships, our working environment becomes dysfunctional.

Due to the many misunderstandings that can lead to unhealthy relationships, unless we are present, low-quality outcomes will dominate our reality. Everywhere you look, if you observe carefully, you will see a great yearning for healthy and wholesome professional relationships in the workplace. Human beings want to feel good in their working environment and, generally speaking, wish to have a good rapport with as many people as possible.

This desire runs through all stages of human development from the baby who seeks to bond with her mother to the teenage boy who wishes to find a girlfriend to the young woman who is fresh out of university and seeks to network with people in the industry she wishes to serve in.

The obvious causes of dysfunctional working relationships are a lack of empathy, a lack of compassion, a lack of open-mindedness and, most importantly, a lack of understanding that sound professional relationships take consistent work. Human beings are not static robots that can remain in one particular mood. A good working relationship takes diligence, vigilance and extra effort.

Just as a thriving business knows that it cannot rest on its laurels, neither can professional relationships. Essentially, it is *people* who make a successful business prosper and if they are in tune with one another and display a good collective spirit, the company has a better chance of thriving.

The compassionate Zen master

The Zen master Thich Nhat Hahn, who was exiled from his native Vietnam, was able to overcome his anger towards inhumane behaviour and completely transcended any ideas of revenge or hostility towards those in his native land.

Rather than resenting the Vietnamese government which refused him entry back into his homeland, as a result of peaceful protests he had a realisation of compassion and developed the habit of mindfulness and empathy. He was able to see that those people who treated him so unjustly were also suffering but, unlike him, were not able to transcend their compulsion for revenge. In his earlier years of campaigning he was able to strike up a friendship with Martin Luther King Jr., who rooted for Thich Nhat Hahn to win the Nobel Peace Prize.

Although Thich Nhat Hahn was not in the business of 'being in business', he created long-lasting relationships with people who were able to build him a global non-profit platform to share his message of peace, understanding and non-violence throughout the world. Had he sought revenge and harboured ill feeling, he would not have attracted the right people to help spread this message and nor would he have been able to create happy relationships with his co-workers and ultimately himself. Perhaps we can take a leaf out of Thich Nhat

Hahn's book and practise enhancing emotional wellbeing, no matter how challenging the circumstances in which we find ourselves.

Exercises

Task 1

Every day (including weekends) for seven days, put a minimum of 20 minutes aside every morning to observe the natural flow of your breathing and watch your thoughts and emotions. Be aware of your chest and stomach rising up and down naturally and notice how your heart is beating effortlessly, just as you breathe without any effort on your behalf. *You may choose to listen to the guided meditations on the MP3 that was included with this course.*

Task 2

When talking to clients, work colleagues, friends or family members, see if you are able to give them your full and undivided attention in the present moment. If you find yourself becoming distracted or drifting off in a conversation, pull yourself back into the present moment. Quite often, many people new to mindfulness discover that they are not as present as they once thought they were, which is a major breakthrough. The more we notice that we are not listening properly or are fixated with our mental commentary (perhaps thinking about our response rather than giving the other person our undivided attention), the quicker we can rectify our lack of mindfulness.

Sometimes, clients have reported to me that, while beginning this mindful communicating practice, they realise old memories and heavy emotions sweep them away from being present if they are in the company of people who trigger them emotionally and remind them of someone who has caused them ill feeling or anxiety in the past.

This realisation is sometimes referred to as transference. Nonetheless, even this can be resolved by coming back to our mindfulness anchor: the life breath. Whether you are making a phone call, exchanging words in the office or having an intense conversation with a client or your co-workers, be present as often as possible.

Task 3

Before you retire in the evening, take a mini self-inventory and answer the following questions. How present were you when communicating with people today? Did you notice anything different in the way you perceived your clients, colleagues, friends and family members? Were you able to give them your undivided attention without being distracted by thoughts and emotions or rehearsing a response while the other person was still speaking? What could you have done better today with respect to your productivity and decision-making? Can you see why it's essential to be fully in the *now* when interacting with other human beings?

Day 1: Reflect and answer the questions.

Day 2: Reflect and answer the questions.

Day 3: Reflect and answer the questions.

Day 4: Reflect and answer the questions.

_____
_____
_____
_____
_____
_____
_____
_____
_____
_____
_____
_____
_____
_____
_____
_____
_____
_____
_____
_____
_____
_____
_____
_____
_____
_____
_____
_____
_____

Day 5: Reflect and answer the questions.

Day 6: Reflect and answer the questions.

_____

_____
_____
_____
_____
_____
_____
_____
_____
_____
_____
_____
_____
_____
_____
_____
_____
_____
_____
_____
_____
_____
_____
_____
_____
_____
_____
_____
_____
_____
_____

Day 7: Reflect and answer the questions.

A Summary of Week 2

Communicating mindfully – what does this mean?

- Being aware of interacting with other people through the use of listening, understanding and open-mindedness
- Being able to appreciate that we all have our differing opinions and perceptions of reality
- Demonstrating empathy and compassion
- Paying attention to people's moods and our own emotions
- Knowing we are human and being able to identify similarities between ourselves and others, whether they are desirable or undesirable qualities
- Giving others our undivided attention

Why is mindful communication essential in the workplace?

- Without communicating in a mindful way, we are more likely to misread situations and come to conclusions which are incorrect and do not serve us. Also, we are more likely to take things personally rather than objectively.
- We run the risk of antagonising colleagues and employees if we do not truly listen.
- Professional relationships require understanding, energy and vigilance; otherwise, they will dissolve and fizzle out.
- We are more likely to demonstrate excellence if we have developed the habit of honouring our relationships with both professionals and clients.

Week 3 –
Focus, Alertness and
Concentration

"When you take your attention into the present moment, a certain
alertness arises. You become more conscious of what's around you,
but also, strangely, a sense of presence that is both within and
without."

— Echart Tolle

All professionals are aware of the necessity to be alert, focused and
maintain a high level of concentration in the workplace. However,
without a mind that is tempered and fully present, internal mental and
external distractions can sweep away focus.

Mistakes are part of the human condition and can help our brain to
grow and develop. However, too many mistakes or a regular pattern of
foolish choices can create chaos. Our lives literally depend on not
making foolish decisions and so does our professional career.

It has been said that the definition of insanity is repeating the same behaviour over and over again and expecting a different result. How many times have we permitted ourselves to entertain a lack of focus and alertness and how many times have we been in denial about our actions?

The intention in any professional life ought to be to make the wisest choices possible and minimise irrational decisions. If we can seriously commit to this, our professional, personal and social lives will improve tremendously.

As with all competence, the process of improving focus, alertness and concentration is a step-by-step plan of subtle action. This is why, in the book *Mindfulness Meditation: Bringing Mindfulness into Everyday Life*, I wrote: "The more attention you pay to the most subtle tasks you undertake throughout the day, the more you will set a vibrational frequency of excellence which flows into whatever you do".

No one can ever reach perfection; however, we can manifest excellence. This is by no means an easy task but it is certainly possible.

Being calm and alert in an alien environment

Since the beginning of time, human beings have had to move out of their comfort zone in order to survive. This has been the case ever since we evolved from being hunter-gatherers, to the axial age, through the age of agriculture, the industrial age, the information age and the current age of advanced technology.

These changes would have caused most people terrible discomfort during the transitional periods from one era to the next. It is very likely that the people who were not able to temper their emotions and evolve during these significant transformations in the way humanity progressed found themselves left behind.

All professionals are aware that new challenges and different working environments can feel 'alien' and create feelings of discomfort, stress and even fear.

In the workplace, it is crucial to be open-minded to any changes taking place which are essential to the cycle of evolution. The new age of phenomenal technology has meant that some industries have suffered or become virtually non-existent and new fields have emerged, bringing with them new opportunities for innovation and productivity.

The person who remains calm and alert during such evolutionary changes will be able to flow and remain emotionally resilient through challenging and difficult times. The writer Eric Hoffer describes this process of evolution in the following way: "In times of change learners inherit the earth while the learned find themselves beautifully equipped to deal with a world that no longer exists".

In order to flow with the constant cycle of change, a steadiness and evenness of mind must be realised, otherwise we will be swimming against the tide. Below are common traits that focused, alert and emotionally grounded people demonstrate most of the time.

- They have an ability to accept how life is unfolding without desperately trying to manipulate outcomes. They are able to emotionally process challenges.
- They have consciously or unconsciously adopted the attitude of 'change the things I can and accept the things I cannot'.
- They are able to detach from the world by taking regular downtime and playtime in a safe manner in an environment that promotes ease and comfort.
- Calm and focused people usually meditate on a daily basis or participate in an activity that promotes mental and emotional wellbeing.
- They are able to demonstrate compassion more easily than people who are habitually angry, quick-tempered or bear grudges.
- They feel connected to their inner source of strength and often feel connected to nature.

- They are assertive but conscious of their behaviour even when they feel angry or disturbed by challenging circumstances.
- They regularly put time aside to reflect and discuss their progress and shortcomings with wise and enlightened mentors.

Being alert and focused

It is much easier to be focused if we are present and not at the mercy of internal or external distractions. A mind that is not sufficiently tempered into the nowness of life will be subject to all sorts of mental activity, which will make it virtually impossible to be focused on our tasks and the objectives at hand.

To be fully focused and committed in our work is to honour the tasks that are in front of us, right now, in the present. Whether we are walking to the other side of the office to hand over a document, making a call to the manager or replying to an email, all tasks, large or small, present an opportunity to build a habit of a focused attitude. Therefore, it makes sense to sharpen our mental muscles to be focused and alert in any and all circumstances.

Being mindful in the workplace

As mentioned in Week 1, mindfulness in the workplace can be realised through developing the habit of regularly noticing that we are breathing. By doing so, we are able to still and silence our repetitive thoughts and be fully present, maintaining clarity in whatever tasks we are working on. Dr Dan Siegel describes it this way: "I look at mindfulness as brain hygiene".

For example, if we have to sit down with a client or work colleague to discuss an important issue, we are going to be far more receptive to their feedback if we are in the 'here and now' with them rather than thinking about which calls need to be made after the meeting or worrying about a stressful business trip the following week. Giving our professional and client-based relationships our undivided attention raises the probability of quality and effectiveness.

This is why in my previous book, *Mindfulness Meditation: Bringing Mindfulness into Everyday Life*, I wrote: "The most efficient way to transcend unsettling thoughts is through the life breath. When we bring our full attention to the life breath, it becomes a gateway to access a deeper and higher level of awareness. We can see our aggressive and disturbing thoughts for what they really are: shallow, short-lived, frequently wrong and at times, comical. Therefore, pay attention to your breathing as often as possible. This is the bedrock to inner peace and tranquility. Anytime you are whisked away by a non-productive or negative thought, focus on your breathing".

Whether we consider ourselves to be religious, spiritual, agnostic or atheist, whatever nationality, race or tribe we are attached to emotionally, whether we work outside, in an office, in a school or at home, we can all breathe and flow into the present moment and, therefore, be alert and focused.

Concentrating

To concentrate and fulfil our objectives requires an alertness and energy. Mental effort is required to concentrate, especially in our professional lives. This quality is imperative and can only be honoured and realised by paying attention to what we are called upon to do in the present moment. If we are continuously pondering and thinking, rather than being present, anxiety and unnecessary errors come into play.

The problem is, by and large, that the workplace has been conditioned to 'mentally force' its way to concentrate, which only tires us out and creates a psychological stagnation in our ability to flow and succeed. To concentrate, we do not need to mentally 'fight' or 'force' our minds to be still. Nor do we need to pump ourselves up with mental aggression to 'get over the line'. None of these methods are effective, and they usually lead to resentment and burnout.

Exercises

Task 1

Continue with your mindfulness meditation practice every morning— watch the life breath flow through you and monitor how quickly your thoughts change from one image to another, observing your emotions and feelings for at least 15 minutes.

After 15 minutes of classic mindfulness meditation, put five minutes aside to focus on a particular object in the room you are sitting in. Whether it is a candle, a vase of flowers or a material object, give it your undivided attention without mentally labelling it. Let us suppose you are observing a vase of flowers: look at it and notice how quickly your mind sweeps you away with thoughts about the past and future, or perhaps thoughts about the day's objectives.

Whenever you notice that you are not fully present while focusing on your chosen object, come back to it. The chances are, if you are a beginner, you will probably only be able to truly observe (without mentally labelling or judging) the object for three to four seconds without being whisked away by your mind.

The more you practise this, the better you will be able to be unconditionally present, which will spill into other areas of your life (especially your professional life). This practice is traditionally called Zen, which is one of the purest and most challenging aspects of mindfulness. Nevertheless, it is one of the most rewarding meditation practices you will undertake. ***You may choose to listen to the*** *guided meditations on the MP3 that was included with this course.*

Task 2

Throughout your day, catch yourself when you are not being fully present and are drifting off into memory, fantasy or speculation. There is a time and a place to visualise new goals, but it is not when we are being asked to focus in the present or are talking to a client or colleague. Stop yourself whenever you notice that your focus, alertness and concentration is lacking. Sometimes this can be due to being hungry or tired. However, more often than not, it is just down to a lack of mindfulness on our part. When all else fails, come back to the life breath and use it as your anchor into the present.

Task 3

Every evening before you retire for the next seven days, take a mini self-appraisal and monitor how your concentration levels have been throughout the day. Answer the following questions honestly:

How would you grade yourself (out of 10) on levels of focus, concentration and alertness? What could you have done differently in your mindfulness day-to-day practice to be more grounded in the present? How often were you truly present in your day-to-day affairs and objectives? Did you catch yourself being swept away by a thought or a heavy emotion or day-dreaming when you should have been concentrating? Are you prepared to put more energy into this practice?

Day 1: Reflect and answer the questions.

Day 2: Reflect and answer the questions.

Day 3: Reflect and answer the questions.

_____
_____
_____
_____
_____
_____
_____
_____
_____
_____
_____
_____
_____
_____
_____
_____
_____
_____
_____
_____
_____
_____
_____
_____
_____
_____
_____
_____
_____
_____
_____
_____
_____
_____

Day 4: Reflect and answer the questions.

Day 5: Reflect and answer the questions.

Day 6: Reflect and answer the questions.

Day 7: Reflect and answer the questions.

A Summary of Week 3

To be focused, alert and to mindfully concentrate – what does this mean?

- To be focused and alert means we are able to mentally and emotionally process our objectives in the present moment.
- To be fully focused on our work is to honour the tasks that are in front of us.
- To mindfully concentrate means we are able to commit ourselves to what needs to be addressed without being diverted by mental distractions and external influences.

Why is it essential to concentrate and remain focused and alert in the workplace?

- Without being focused and alert, we cannot be fully present and effective.
- Mindfully concentrating helps us to minimise our anxieties and errors in the workplace.
- We can avoid added stress and worry by transcending the habit of procrastination.
- We are able to preserve our energy and be more efficient and resilient.

Week 4 –
Mindfulness and Emotional Intelligence

"Emotion has its place, but it must not interfere with taking the appropriate action."

– Susan Oakey-Baker

The long-held general perception that to work on developing emotional intelligence is frothy or 'new-age' and somehow something to be sniggered at is fast becoming outdated. It is increasingly being recognised that emotional intelligence is crucial in order to be able to deal with adversity and challenges.

Someone who repeatedly attempts to bury his or her fearful emotions is kidding themselves. Sooner or later, the suppressed feelings will have to manifest in one way or another.

Many of us have developed certain skills to be effective servants to our clients, community and loving stewards of our family, but we can often miss the mark of maximising our potential as a result of lacking inner composure and serenity. This is why the aforementioned Victorian author James Allen wrote, "Calmness of mind is one of the beautiful jewels of wisdom".

The author of the classic book *Emotional Intelligence*, Daniel Goleman, has dedicated his life to assisting people in how to be emotionally intelligent, calm and explore self-awareness.

Here is what Daniel Goleman wrote about being emotionally steady and mindful: "If your emotional abilities aren't in hand, if you don't have self-awareness, if you are not able to manage your distressing emotions, if you can't have empathy and have effective relationships, then no matter how smart you are, you are not going to get very far".

It would be sensible to make developing emotional intelligence as much of a priority as caring for your physical wellbeing. To be emotionally intelligent in the workplace means that you can observe your emotions and sense the moods of others, tap into your intuitive nature, delay gratification, be able to discriminate and detach from feelings and continuously develop a sound temperament in the present moment.

When the weeks have built up with frustration and immense stress and one of your co-workers, a manager or an employee triggers irritation or angers you, knowing how to respond in a mindful way can pay huge dividends. Knowing how to not take other people's emotional baggage personally and intuitively sensing when to bring up concerns and when not to is an expression of emotional intelligence. This is all possible if we are being truly mindful.

Emotional intelligence is just as important as academic intelligence

More people in mainstream society today are coming to terms with the fact that having a high IQ or being an excellent academic doesn't equate to living a happy, fulfilling and successful life. The debate with respect to defining intelligence is still relevant. Nonetheless, more businesses have realised that emotional intelligence is just as important as academic intelligence, perhaps even more so.

No matter how brilliant a biologist, an economics professor, a corporate accountant or a cardiologist, he/she will not last very long in their field of excellence without cultivating emotional intelligence.

Go back into your memory and consider the people you went to school with. Consider the students who displayed an excellent IQ or a brilliant academic mind. How many of them today are mentally and emotionally well and are thriving in a career of their personal choice?

The fact is that IQ plays a smaller part in success than other components such as health (especially a nutritious diet and nurturing in the first five years of early development), luck, mindfulness, social upbringing, social intelligence, early childhood imprinting (habits, thoughts and beliefs impressed on us by parents or guardians), environment, birthplace and emotional intelligence.

Emotional intelligence and mindfulness can easily compensate for not having an IQ of 160. The challenges and conflicts encountered in a professional life that come from interacting with other human beings can often be resolved through empathy, compassion, controlling impulses, understanding (being able to see things from the other person's point of view) and emotional regulation; in other words, all of the elements of emotional intelligence.

Awareness of emotion

To be mindful and emotionally steady in one's consciousness and to demonstrate composure means that you respect your feelings but are not inclined to believe that they are the ultimate truth.

Some people find this extremely hard to accept and feel that their emotions must be expressed at all times, even in the workplace, but this is a counterproductive way to behave.

Sometimes our feelings signify clarity and sometimes they are distorted due to an inaccurate perspective imprinted on the human mind. Human emotions can be delicate and without a steady calmness to be alert, present and in-tune with how we and other people feel, we will make it extremely difficult for us to be effective professionals. All wise men and women have come to realise that to be serene, considerate and tolerant is not just a matter of adopting virtues, but is essential in order to bring harmony and equanimity into human relationships.

It is important to point out that no one can truly make a rational decision without the emotional brain being activated in some way. Even the person who is most effective at maintaining clarity of thought will base his/her decision on some measure of feeling. In other words, the idea that we can make decisions which are purely rational is a misnomer.

Human beings are not robotic machines—our minds and brains are phenomenally complex. Practising mindfulness can enable us to achieve a healthy balance between intellect and emotion, which is a key component of emotional intelligence.

Emotionally steady

To be emotionally steady does not mean that we deny how we feel or that we are called upon to suppress our emotions. This approach would only repress our mental and emotional development, in the same way that someone might resort to sedating themselves with drugs or alcohol whenever they feel anxious or fearful about an unaddressed issue. His/her emotional and mental growth would thus be greatly handicapped.

To be steady irrespective of our emotions, we have to feel and honour our emotions without suppressing them even if they are painful, knowing that they will pass and allow our awareness to observe and monitor how we are feeling. With emotional intelligence, we know how to behave appropriately and are demonstrating a mindful approach to professionalism.

How many times have you behaved in a manner which you would not wish to repeat today? Wouldn't a more desirable outcome have been achieved had you been able to restrain the actions or words, which subsequently caused you and others discomfort?

A human being who demonstrates stability and calmness will respect the cycle of emotional ups and downs and will concede to the fact that equilibrium lies underneath emotion. All we have to do to access such awareness (an awareness that is ultimately neutral to how we feel) is to rise above our feelings and observe our thought patterns, beliefs and habits.

Transcending ill feeling, resentments, grudges and revenge

The Chinese philosopher and wisdom teacher Confucius declared: "Before you embark on a journey of revenge, dig two graves". Similarly, Nelson Mandela said, "Resentment is like drinking poison and then hoping it will kill your enemies".

Both these statements hold immense truth and great wisdom. When we harbour ill feeling towards someone at work, home or anywhere else for that matter, we stifle creativity and prevent ourselves from fully concentrating and giving our undivided attention to the tasks at hand in the present moment. We are more likely to burn out if we are charged with anger, fear or feelings of being 'hard done by'.

A person consumed by bitterness and animosity becomes a liability because their mind is distorted with a bleak perception of reality. They are allowing their brainstem, their limbic area and the subcortical sphere of their brain to dominate their emotional state rather than directing their prefrontal cortex to enforce emotional intelligence and rationality.

Sadly, many societies tolerate revenge and encourage harbouring bad feeling towards people we perceive to have harmed us, but the truth is that if we harbour toxic feelings we attract unpleasant circumstances and start to damage our mental, emotional and physical health.

Letting go of pointless mental distractions

Many scientists and doctors fully subscribe to the idea that harbouring ill feeling is not good for our physiology or our mental and emotional wellbeing. When we resent a colleague or client for their behaviour (or maybe because of their success), we lose the opportunity to enjoy the present moment. Many people hold onto grudges for years and then wonder why they are more often than not unhappy and feel despondent.

It is important to keep in mind that the person we resent is probably getting on with their life while we simmer with these toxic emotions. The idea that revenge fuels ambition and drive is a myth.

We are far more likely to accomplish our professional goals, display initiative and get on better with colleagues and clients if we are not harbouring egoism but are instead genuinely enjoying our craft while fostering a healthy long-term vision and a desire to persist.

We could all find examples of people who have gathered some measure of prestige or 'success' by making themselves believe that the world is out to get them ('me against everyone else'), but if you were to study their personal biographies or monitor their behaviour you might find that they were plagued by unhappiness, anger and egomania.

Releasing anger

The question is this: what do we do when our anger towards a colleague or a client is so intense that we feel a compulsive need to retaliate?

Naturally, mindfulness is always the first option. To amplify the practice of present-moment-awareness, find a scrap piece of paper and a pen. Then do the following:

- Take seven deep breaths, breathing in for a count of seven seconds and breathing out for a count of nine seconds.

- List all the feelings you have towards this person or group of people.
- No matter how extreme the emotions you are describing, write them down, remembering that no one else will read this.
- Once you have released the toxic emotions on paper, take another deep breath and rip the paper into shreds.
- Next ask the question, 'How can I let go of this negative emotion?' While reflecting on this question, remind yourself that people tend to behave due to their conditioning. All of us, to some degree, are a reflection of our environment.
- Keep in mind that our perception of reality will shape how we view other people. This is why the writer and teacher Wayne Dyer advises us to "Change the way you look at things, and the things you look at change".

The next time someone sends you an email or text message which triggers inner rage and anger, or the next time a work colleague or client talks to you in a tone you feel is unsuitable for creating harmony, follow the suggestions above.

It is very difficult to remain angry with someone when we recognise that we may have, at some point, behaved in a similar way. Similarly, it is virtually impossible to feel hostile towards someone if we have developed an ability to feel empathy, compassion and understanding. Imagine how many difficulties at work could be resolved as a result of a slight shift in perception, attitude and awareness?

All wise people know that, in order to fully capitalise on our talents and skills, we must be frank with ourselves and identify the personal shortcomings that prevent our talents and skills from being maximised.

Ask yourself: is there someone you resent? Do you feel hostility towards someone you are working with? Do you resent a client? Do competitive markets or rival businesses trigger anger and inner rage?

Are you envious of anyone in the workplace? Be very honest with yourself and if you find that you have been harbouring these feelings, make a choice to do something to temper them.

For example, the next time you feel negative emotions towards someone at work, even if you do not mean it at the first attempt, without saying it out loud, wish the person peace of mind and happiness.

If you wish to master toxic feelings, developing the habit of wishing others well will make this possible. At first, you might grudgingly repeat these words. Nevertheless, in a reasonably short period of time, you will genuinely feel in a place of neutrality in their presence and will be able to detach from negative emotions. You might not even like them, but by wishing the person well, you become free from investing your emotional health into someone else's actions.

Once you are able to demonstrate this practice of wishing good things for people, you will feel more confident and calm in the way you approach people and will be emotionally resilient to challenges. In other words, angry and bitter emotions weaken us on all levels. To store ill feeling in the body is like holding a hot piece of metal in our hands and refusing to let go of it.

Remember that anyone can scream, shout, whine and bad-mouth others, but it calls for extra courage and inner strength to act better than we feel and override the reptilian emotions that tempt us to reciprocate and hit back.

Awareness before picking up the phone or sending an email or text message

An excellent practice that we can apply without disrupting our fluency in the workplace is to be consciously present in the moment before making a phone call or responding to an email or other communication.

For instance, rather than rushing to make a call, give yourself three seconds to remind yourself that you are breathing. Similarly, this practice can be realised after receiving a call or email. We can consciously breathe for several seconds, allowing our minds to calm. This practice will help to eliminate any tendency to 'react' to a potential problem rather than 'respond' to it. How many times have we sent a hasty reply to someone and then later regretted it?

After a while, these mini mindfulness meditations become habitual and relieve us from the constant stream of thinking.

Jealousy clutters the mind and destroys calmness

A destructive emotion which would be wise to guard against at all costs is 'jealousy'. This toxic emotion seriously damages our emotional health, human relationships and sense of belonging. It is detrimental to our capacity to maximise our potential. It is also an emotion which most of us are very reluctant to admit to.

No one can be calm and mindful without freeing themselves from this unfortunate mental state. It eats away at us, burdens us with a painful heaviness in our bodies, diminishes our capacity to succeed and steals our happiness. Extreme cases of this emotion cause people to kill, but even subtle day-to-day expressions of this emotion are enough to destroy any team spirit or good relationships with clients.

Some people are so consumed by this emotion that they are completely at its mercy. They take pleasure in talking about the shortcomings of the people they envy when they themselves haven't addressed their own issues. This is why Confucius said, "Don't complain about the snow on your neighbour's roof when you have snow on yours".

Jealousy is the illusion of losing something that you do not own. It is irrational to be jealous of someone because they have something that you 'think' you want. Even worse, it engenders a false belief that what you have is not enough. This concept is driven by the human ego and creates a perception of scarcity and a false sense of injustice.

Distorted awareness creates envy

Ordinarily, 'jealousy' can be expressed as fear of loss, loneliness and even distrust. Parul Sehgal was absolutely spot on when she said: "When we feel jealous, we tell ourselves a story. We tell ourselves a story about other people's lives. These stories make us feel terrible because they are designed to make us feel terrible. As the teller of the tale and the audience, we know just what details to include to dig that knife in".

If you seriously consider that statement along with the other realisations in this book about jealousy, you would have to agree that it is a form of self-harm which slips under the radar in mainstream society due to it being a common affliction in millions of people's lives, creating untold emotional and mental scars.

The next time you are consumed by this unattractive emotion, rather than indulging it through destructive thoughts, feelings and behaviour or by saying regrettable things, take a personal inventory and discuss these shortcomings with a trusted friend.

The reality is that most of us have, at some stage of our lives, suffered from jealousy. There is nothing to be embarrassed or ashamed about.

Weekly phone calls that release jealousy

Jealousy used to be a real handicap for me. The emotion had become so deeply ingrained in me from a young age that I was not even aware of how seriously it was affecting my actions and behaviour.

When I reached a point where I had to address it since it was causing me much suffering, I embarked on the process of self-appraisals and sharing these undesirable feelings with trusted friends. This, however, was not enough and more action was required.

First of all, I started to mentally wish people well as suggested earlier on. Then, one day, a spontaneous conversation took place with a friend that led to the two of us agreeing to call one another several times a week, every week, and read out a list of people we wished to direct kind thoughts towards (usually people we had previously harboured envious feelings towards). The intention of this practice was to diminish any lingering envious emotions and to develop a steady habit of automatically wishing people well. This helped us to develop the habit of sabotaging envious emotions, which are nothing more than suppressed fear and a lack of mindfulness.

On some occasions, several names were repeated over and over again until no more ill feeling could be felt towards them. We then compounded the exercise by expressing gratitude for that person.

The point is that the two of us were developing new qualities that were suitable for harmonious and successful living. I cannot speak for my friend (although I am certain he felt the same as I did), but incredible shifts in my awareness started to blossom during the one-year practice of calling each other every week to transcend envy and jealousy.

I started to feel good about people who used to bother me. Therefore, I had more mental space to channel positive feelings into productive activities rather than being consumed with emotional toxicity. I noticed that people started to respond to me differently.

Ill feeling in the workplace

People who are mindful and have equanimity within themselves have no need to feel spite towards their work colleagues. They know that to resent their co-workers, partners, shareholders or chairman will only fill their minds with negativity and cannot possibly bear any good long-term fruit.

The Wisdom Traditions emphasised this: "Anger will never disappear so long as thoughts of resentment are cherished in the mind. Anger will disappear just as soon as thoughts of resentment are forgotten".

Therefore, be honest with yourself. Do you take a perverse pleasure in seeing people suffer, especially people who you perceive to be more effective than you or who are, perhaps, not quite as intellectually gifted as you? If this is the case, know that you can decide not to participate in such a self-destructive attitude anymore.

If we wish our work colleagues or employees or employers to treat us with respect and kindness we must behave this way first. This is why Mahatma Gandhi said: "Be the change you wish to see in the world", while the Greek philosopher, Socrates, said: "Be as you wish to seem". Thus, the theory of the Golden Rule can be your foundation for being an effective worker: "Do unto others as you would have them do onto you".

With this principle firmly embedded in your heart and mind, trust and genuine appreciation are sure to follow you wherever you go. No one likes to be on the receiving end of unfriendly behaviour and if you can avoid behaving in such a way, your professional relationships will greatly improve in the long term.

Addressing pugnacious personalities when the chips are down

Let's face it. Some people are manically driven to be antagonistic and cannot help but have their 'say', often at the expense of the collective harmony of the group. They try to pass on their unresolved childhood trauma, unaddressed anger and shame issues and lack of self-worth. How many business meetings are disrupted by difficult personalities?

If someone attempts to put us down (to fuel their sense of self-worth), it is their own fear, shame and guilt that they are trying to pass on to us.

Unfortunately, some people will never change their habits. The fact is that not everyone cares to develop their character or emotional intelligence, let alone be mindful and communicate better with colleagues. What at first might be exasperating is the realisation that we cannot avoid colleagues or clients who display arrogance and narcissism in working environments.

One of the most common complaints in the workplace that has come to my attention is the difficulty people find in working with narrow-minded individuals, regardless if it is with an obnoxious and arrogant boss or an employee or client with a sense of entitlement.

If resentments towards difficult co-workers and clients are left unchecked, a good-spirited employee or employer will become disheartened with their work and, sooner or later, their performance will be below their usual standards. This is a recipe for disaster in a working environment and will take its toll on creativity, innovation and financial profit in the long run.

In his book, *Healing The Shame That Binds You*, John Bradshaw wrote: "Arrogance or pride is defined as offensively exaggerating one's own importance. The proud, arrogant person alters her mood by means of her exaggeration".

If we consider Bradshaw's perspective (which I fully subscribe to) on an arrogant person trying to constantly alter the way he or she feels, we have an opportunity to release any ill feeling towards them.

In other words, this person is suffering mentally and emotionally and cannot feel comfortable in his or her own skin. As a result, they attempt to make themselves feel better by feeling they are 'better' than everyone else, which manifests as ugly and unattractive behaviour. This becomes a vicious cycle as they are completely entrapped by their habit.

But how do we maintain emotional resilience and deal with brash personalities, especially when the chips are down? Thankfully, there is a simple solution to this common challenge and that is to practise compassion and understanding. With compassion, empathy and understanding, these unattractive characteristics will no longer bother you. You will not take their behaviour personally and will be able to rise above thoughts of retaliation.

Naturally, unacceptable behaviour in the workplace cannot be condoned, but the underlying resentment towards dysfunctional behaviour can be rapidly transformed into feelings of compassion. Questions such as, 'I wonder what suffering he or she has gone through that makes him or her behave like that?' can greatly help us to transgress any undesirable emotions such as anger or vengefulness.

As expressed earlier on in this book, being angry will handicap our professional progress in the long run. If we do not develop empathy and understanding, we are always vulnerable to resentment, which weakens our judgement and position.

The reality is that some men and women are so determined to get what they want that they will do almost anything to get it, even at the cost of their own dignity and self-respect and will gladly step on the toes of their fellows to advance.

They are like parasites because, although they might show initiative, cleverness and have an abundance of energy, they lack genuine integrity and wisdom and make life uncomfortable for the rest of us, who are working within certain ethical boundaries. Quite often, although not in all cases, people who display such unattractive qualities will be big-shots and egomaniacs who deliberately 'rock the boat' without any sound reason for doing so. As Shakespeare pointed out centuries ago, "Man, proud man, dressed in a little brief authority plays such fantastic tricks before high heaven and makes the angels weep".

Pathological competitiveness

In today's culture, an over-emphasis on being driven and competitive has become so deeply ingrained in people's minds that they are quite unaware of being that way and consider it to be the 'the norm'.

The notion of creating harmony amongst colleagues is often dismissed by many employees who see this as a 'weakness' and are so desperately competitive that they unconsciously encourage friction in the working environment. They forget that they reap what they sow and that, if they create disharmony for others, unwelcome reactions will eventually catch up with them, even if it is many years down the line.

In the world of business, one cannot get away from the fact that other businesses will be providing a similar service or product which drives competition and can fuel productivity. However, when competition becomes a relentless power trip, unwelcome outcomes can manifest.

History suggests that a mass eruption of greed will manifest several times a century. One only has to look at the insanity of the global financial crisis in 2008 to observe the gross immorality and greed that was rampant in some of the biggest financial institutions.

It is healthy to wish to improve and to advance in our careers but all wise and successful men and women know that we cannot get very far in life without harmony, cooperation and a positive attitude towards those we encounter in our professional lives.

It is far easier to accomplish our goals if we are emotionally composed and able to flow into mindfulness rather than being consumed by anxiety and worrying that others are going to 'overtake us'.

Admitting our mistakes and taking responsibility

By admitting our shortcomings, we open a channel to improve and hopefully not to repeat the same behaviour again. This is a great challenge in the collective workforce. Do enough of us promptly admit when we have missed the mark without seeking to blame others?

Many of us will blame our mistakes on others and when we are subject to disciplinary action, we may resent the person disciplining us. If we are not able to admit our faults to ourselves and others, how can we possibly learn from them? To deny our errors is to prevent improvement and neglect emotional intelligence.

Some of us are able to concede to our shortcomings but then go on to use this as a self-harm device to wallow in self-pity and morbid reflection. This is not a healthy approach either. If we have made a mistake at work, first of all, let us not blame anyone else and secondly let us not be too hard on ourselves and see that learning from our mistakes is a necessary part of growth.

Thus, we have the saying 'to err is human'; we cannot avoid it. All in all, people tend to respect those who can own their shortcomings and who make the effort to improve. Such actions demonstrate humility and are admired amongst the wise.

The six mistakes

The Roman philosopher and lawyer Marcus Cicero believed that the common shortcomings of humanity are a result of a frame of mind. Below are what Marcus Cicero named 'the six mistakes mankind keeps making century after century'. As you digest the bullet points below, see if you concur with Cicero's observations on human folly.

- Believing that personal gain is made by crushing others
- Worrying about things that cannot be changed or corrected
- Insisting that a thing is impossible because we cannot accomplish it
- Refusing to set aside trivial preferences
- Neglecting development and refinement of the mind
- Attempting to compel others to believe and live as we do

How much more effective would we be in the workplace if we could transcend the shortcomings listed above by Marcus Cicero?

Persist and observe your emotions

Whenever your emotions are disturbed, ride the wave and gently persist. Just as you may not feel like making that extra phone call or sending a long email to a client, you can override this emotion with awareness (not intellect); as a result of being mindful, you will benefit from taking action.

Your potential to be an excellent employer or employee is great once you fully understand that a major obstacle stopping you from being highly effective is allowing your emotions to dictate your behaviour and attitude. Overriding these emotions whenever possible will reap untold rewards.

Many of us go through major changes in our careers. Some of us have been working in a particular field for decades but find ourselves drawn to something new. Others are asked to move abroad by our company and adapt to a new culture. Offices close and new ones open. Managers come and go and companies frequently merge and change direction.

One thing is clear in the 21st Century; instability in the workplace is certain. Whatever our circumstance and however they may differ, change is inevitable and learning to be emotionally intelligent and mindful is essential. There is no doubt that emotional intelligence and mindfulness are necessary throughout all stages of our careers, regardless of whether we remain in one particular industry or branch out into something completely new.

The characteristics that prevent effectiveness

- A lack of mindfulness and capacity to be fully present in the moment
- Neglecting to train the prefrontal cortex to integrate empathetic and efficient behaviour

- Harbouring ill feeling, resentment, grudges and compulsively seeking revenge
- Having a spiteful attitude and wishing harm upon others
- Being pathologically competitive and prepared to do anything to advance (including neglecting an ethical approach)
- A jealous and envious attitude
- A lack of compassion and understanding
- A lack of open-mindedness and tolerance
- A habit of criticising, blaming, feeling like a victim and wallowing in self-pity and morbid reflection
- A lack of integrity and humility

Once these negative characteristics are replaced with higher qualities, our professional lives will dramatically improve and our work ethic and capacity to serve will be greatly enhanced. Our personal and social lives will also take a dramatic turn for the better.

For the next seven days, honour the following tasks and know in your heart that you have fully committed yourself to the exercises.

Exercises

Task 1

Continue with your mindfulness meditation practice every morning. Observe the life breath but give particular attention to your emotional state for 20 minutes. Notice how you are feeling without questioning why you are feeling that way. Just be the awareness behind the emotion and enjoy breathing. This will help you to develop awareness of your feelings throughout the day without being disturbed by emotional turbulence. *You may choose to listen to the guided meditations on the MP3 that was included with this course.*

Task 2

Throughout the day, observe your emotional state. Identify when your emotions are either elevating your performance or throwing you off course. These observations will help us to see that our emotions can hijack our ability to be of maximum service. Whether we feel flat or upbeat, we can still perform our duty in a satisfactory way.

Be aware of other people's moods without over-analysing. See if you can sense when a colleague or client has a heaviness or lightness in their mood. This practice will sharpen our intuitive and instinctive abilities.

Task 3

Before you retire at night, for the next seven days, take another self-appraisal and reflect honestly on how you have tempered your emotions. If there are specific examples that you would like to write down, do so. Answer the following questions:

What emotions have been the dominant forces in your day? If you experienced any heavy or negative emotions, did you manage to transcend them? If you have experienced upbeat and positive emotions, did you cultivate them? Were you able to pick up on the moods of fellow co-workers or clients? Did your feelings prevent you from delivering your objectives and, if so, what could you have done better? If you were to grade yourself (on a scale of 1–10), how has your emotional intelligence and mindful practice been today?

Day 1: Reflect and answer the questions.

Day 2: Reflect and answer the questions.

Day 3: Reflect and answer the questions.

_____

_____

_____

_____

_____

_____

_____

_____

_____

_____

_____

_____

_____

_____

_____

_____

_____

_____

_____

_____

_____

_____

_____

_____

_____

_____

_____

_____

_____

Day 4: Reflect and answer the questions.

_____
_____
_____
_____
_____
_____
_____
_____
_____
_____
_____
_____
_____
_____
_____
_____
_____
_____
_____
_____
_____
_____
_____
_____
_____
_____
_____
_____
_____

Day 5: Reflect and answer the questions.

Day 6: Reflect and answer the questions.

Day 7: Reflect and answer the questions.

A Summary of Week 4

To be emotionally intelligent – what does this mean?

- Being able to manage your emotions during vicissitudes— to make a conscious effort to be emotionally steady as often as possible
- To be in tune with your own and other people's emotions, meaning you can communicate from a place of empathy and compassion
- To have an awareness (to *be* the awareness) that can differentiate between thoughts and emotions
- Being able to mindfully balance intellect and emotion
- Having self-awareness and being able to recognise an emotion as it arises in the present moment
- Being able to channel your emotional energy in an intelligent way without being exhausted
- Developing the habit of making an intention every morning to be calm and not let ourselves be drawn into other people's drama or emotional triggers

Why is emotional intelligence imperative in the workplace?

- Success and effectiveness can be enhanced and developed by your being able to monitor and manage your emotions and feelings in the workplace.
- Without emotional intelligence and mindfulness, we are more likely to behave in unemotional, intelligent ways and lose our centre point (our grounded emotional state). With the challenges of constant contact with other human

beings (who also have their emotions to deal with), life in general can be too overwhelming and stressful without emotional intelligence.

- Emotional intelligence and mindfulness make leadership and managing other people possible.
- Emotional intelligence is now being recognised as an essential quality needed to thrive and succeed in the 21st Century.

Week 5 –
Emotional Resilience

"Adversity opens the door to resilience."

– Eileen Rockefeller Growald

When life throws difficulties at us and the mind is restless, emotional resilience will see us through challenging times. We can work through tempestuous emotions and self-doubt and come through them unharmed and avoid self-sabotage and self-harm.

Week 5 focuses on emotional resilience, which can be cultivated through mindful practice and other meditation techniques. By and large, all human beings are naturally resilient. However, emotional resilience is an asset which must be developed and consistently monitored. Even the great Zen masters who have dedicated their entire lives to being unconditionally present in the moment have had to develop emotional resilience in order to persist in their extremely difficult rituals.

The fact is that we are going to experience emotional pain and hurt on a regular basis. We cannot escape this. Once we accept this fact, pain and suffering no longer become personal or diminish our self-worth. Thus, we realise that pain is necessary to the human journey. When setbacks occur and when our plans are undermined, we can flow and quickly rejuvenate our spirit with optimism, reflection and rationality without being thrown off course or sinking into despondency or despair.

Letting go of negative mental stories

The Greek philosopher Aristotle once said "It is the mark of an educated mind to be able to entertain a thought without accepting it". What exactly did he mean by that? To be aware means that we are fully aware of our own awareness. Imagine what would happen if we developed the habit of not taking things personally at work and remained emotionally resilient. How would our productivity and focus improve? The mental stories that we tell ourselves have the power to enhance or sabotage our wellbeing. The art is to realise that mental stories are simply thoughts, beliefs and memories. Once we know this, we are free from our mental shackles.

An employee might have developed new skills and qualities to succeed in the workplace, but because she is fixated on previous difficulties and disappointments, she panics and feels that she will not be able to cope. Similarly, many of us have felt anxious and afraid when our professional lives take a turn for the better due to negative memories. Thoughts such as 'This is too difficult', 'I'm afraid of missing this deadline', 'What if I fail?' and 'What if my contract is terminated?' can recycle themselves continuously until we feel emotionally drained and are utterly consumed with tension.

The sad truth is that millions of competent and otherwise brilliant human beings are limited by the mental shackles in the mind.

The mental commentary and persistent anxious thoughts trap them into reliving the same emotions and behavioural patterns. Their history and personalised biographies prevent them from being free and liberated. Many of us have a private cinema in our minds that projects terrifying imaginary outcomes and a constant stream of memories of loss and discord.

The mental monologues are so potent and powerful that, unless we can anchor ourselves in the present and break the spell of compulsive thinking, we are trapped. The truth is that most of our day-to-day worries, fears and concerns are highly unlikely to manifest and so many hours are squandered in unnecessary suffering.

The only solution that I have found after years of research and unrelenting practice is to make a commitment to train myself to operate in the present moment as often as possible. Positive self-talk and motivational techniques can be helpful but the long-term solution to transcend our negative mental commentary is to be present.

The author and teacher Nanice Ellis complements the realisation of letting go of mental stories with the following wise words: "Stories like 'he must not care' or 'if she loved me, she wouldn't have done this,' are the breeding ground for so much sorrow. Most of the time, the stories that we tell ourselves and believe, have more to do with our own personal history, rather than the actual relationship that seems to be the cause".

Develop the habit of being calm and emotionally resilient

It took 15 years for Albert Einstein's theory of relatively to be widely accepted. Vicissitudes galore disrupted his professional progress, including the break out of the Great War, having to revise his theory just months before it was embraced by the world and experiencing grave personal problems with his family. He remained persistent in his efforts through all of these harrowing events, however, and was known for sitting in silence for hours, days and sometimes weeks, reflecting and being mindful of his thought processes and emotions, remaining deeply in the present moment.

We all have moments when we feel like packing everything in and 'disappearing'. This is our mind and body telling us that we have reached a mental and emotional turning point and we should therefore go easy on ourselves. Extreme stress or compounded disheartening circumstances can lead to even the most resilient of professionals burning out or perhaps even considering quitting their careers.

A dose of the present moment, however, recharges our emotional battery and cleanses our mind from toxic thoughts and draining concerns. This is why, in the book *Mindfulness Meditation: Bringing Mindfulness into Everyday Life*, I wrote: "Imagine a drawing board with all of our guilt, shame and dysfunctional thoughts written on them, which are a projection of the future or a collection of our past memories. When we step into the present moment (the nowness of consciousness), the board is wiped completely clean".

Emotional resilience can be learnt at any age. However, the sooner we learn to develop this desirable quality, the more likely it is to become a habit that we have incorporated into our behaviour. Thus the saying "The chains of habit are too light to be felt until they are too heavy to be broken".

With this foundation properly in place, it is easier to build a long-term enjoyable career and be emotionally resilient. What are some of these habits? Let us take a look below.

Letting go of the outcome

It is impossible to control outcomes or results, although most of us have been programmed from a very young age to believe otherwise. The idea that we can perform actual 'magic' causes tremendous dysfunction, unnecessary suffering and prevents the development of emotional resilience.

We can exert some degree of control over our efforts and attitude, but the outcome of these efforts is out of our hands.

For instance, consider someone who has diligently studied the stock market for decades and has applied himself in order to understand how to value a business. He may have had many occasions of triumphs and glory but then, due to a blind spot or an unexpected disaster in the stock market, he loses millions of pounds. The outcome was not in his hands.

Or consider a social worker who has developed priceless skills such as understanding and compassion. She might have been working diligently to assist a man who has serious mental health problems and has no family but requires assistance for living accommodation. She has been assisting him for months and feels she is making progress with the local government to push his case forward. Then one day, she comes into work and finds out that the man she was helping has committed suicide. What then?

Similarly, look at the unpredictability of the world of sport. A competent football manager in the English Premier League may have built a solid, creative and efficient football team. His players are on a good run with eight consecutive wins and his team are about to face a competitor who has come off the back of losing three games on the trot. However, the evening before match day, his best player has an injury and subsequently during the match day two of his top players are sent off, causing a string of random events on the pitch which lead to his team being humiliated and losing the game to a weaker side.

Things sometimes go our way and sometimes they don't. All we can do is apply ourselves to our profession, giving our very best effort but emotionally letting go of the outcome. Why? Because if we obsess about an outcome, we cannot possibly honour the present moment.

In other words, rather than honouring the present moment and giving our focus and complete and undivided attention to our work, we stress ourselves out and operate in a state of fear and worry about an outcome that may or may not materialise. Such an unhealthy approach damages our mental and emotional wellbeing.

If we study the great Wisdom Traditions (particularly the Eastern Wisdom Traditions), there is a great emphasis on not attempting to control results. Naturally, we must plan and apply ourselves to our profession and our vision but the most important factor is what is happening right here, right now. What we create in the present moment flows into the future so let us be in an alert, relaxed state as we go through the process of working.

On the Teen Ink YouTube video channel, writer, musician and philanthropist Peter Buffett was interviewed by an audience with respect to his journey into success and finding his purpose. A teenage girl asked Peter Buffett what was the most important life lesson he had learnt from his father Warren Buffett, the aforementioned financial investor and teacher. He replied, with respect to his father: "He's just not attached to an outcome. While following your passion is important, not being attached to the outcome might be more important, because then you're not predetermining where you might go or what might happen—you're just present in what you're doing and trying to be the best at it or the most effective or whatever it might be. And so, I would say that's probably the greatest lesson I learnt from both my parents, quite honestly, is to not be attached to the outcome of something".

If you intend to strengthen your emotional resilience muscles (which is essential to being successful and emotionally well), developing the habit of letting go of the outcome is imperative.

The habits of emotionally resilient professionals

- A habit of thoroughly enjoying being of service and having an appreciation for the work one does
- A habit of doing more than is expected (no one can truly excel by doing just enough to stay employed)
- A habit of wishing people well and expelling feelings of jealousy and greed from one's consciousness

- A habit of practising mindfulness meditation for at least 20 minutes every morning and taking time to reflect on one's attitude and activities before retiring at night
- A habit of remembering to breathe properly and to pause throughout the day—breathing deeply into stillness
- A habit of training the brain to be emotionally intelligent
- A habit of expressing genuine gratitude for the positive and negative experiences in life
- An open mind and a willingness to move with the times, even if it causes emotional pain and a feeling of discomfort
- A habit of being mindful of one's thoughts, feelings and behaviours—an awareness of what is happening in the present moment and an ability to observe events with clarity

An exercise on characteristics that lead to effectiveness

If you were to meditate and reflect on five people you admire who are effective, emotionally resilient and have healthy and friendly relationships in professional, personal and social settings, what qualities do they possess? They probably make an effort to show a genuine appreciation for other people's interests and philosophies; they are open-minded, so to speak.

Another part of this exercise is to reflect on the characteristics of five people who you would certainly not wish to spend any time with (if you had the power to choose who you associate with). Perhaps they are dishonest, extremely self-centred, lazy or untrustworthy.

If you identify any one of the unattractive characteristics listed in the people you do not resonate with in your own personality now is the time to release them from your attitude. You do not need to behave in an ugly way as long as you are willing to transcend old behavioural patterns and develop new empowering habits.

Bear in mind that we cannot think our way out of negative actions but we can act our way out of destructive perspectives and thought patterns. The process of changing habits is a gradual daily activity. Sir William Osler, the author of the classic book *A Way of Life*, wrote, "Our main business is not to see what lies dimly at a distance, but to do what lies clearly at hand".

Recent scientific findings on neuroplasticity show that repetition of behaviour, thoughts, emotions and even new experiences shapes our entire demeanour and affects our brain. Harvard professor, and co-author of the book *Super Brain*, Rudolph E. Tanzi said: "When you have a new experience, you are changing the neural network of your brain at various levels".

Similarly, Albert Einstein once famously suggested that we can experience many things we wish by developing the right habits. Einstein said: "Match the frequency of the reality you want and you cannot help but get that reality. It can be no other way. This is not philosophy. This is physics".

By adopting this practical mindful approach and by applying yourself to the exercises in Week 5, you will start the process of creating new neural networks in your brain, which will gradually transform your entire reality and assist you to be a resilient professional.

Whenever you consciously reinforce a new behaviour, new habits are formed which will either bring evolutionary or destructive outcomes, not just professionally but in your life as a whole.

By and large, it takes 30 days to create a foundation for a new habit. Subsequently, it is just a case of keeping momentum and remaining vigilant until the behaviour is habitual. This is how mindfulness becomes a wonderful practice while we develop and monitor desirable qualities that lead to success.

Self-acceptance and self-awareness lead to emotional resilience

Once we have self-awareness and are able to be honest with ourselves, we come to realise that emotions change and our feelings can alter very quickly. So often, when we are feeling good, we want it to last forever, which is obviously not possible. Nonetheless, we cling and attach ourselves to feelings of happiness and joy, which leads to a greater emotional shock when opposite feelings such as anger and fear arise.

If we cling on to any emotion, we weaken our chances of being emotionally resilient. This is where self-acceptance comes into play in our professional lives. Once we accept that we are going to have emotionally challenging times as well as more rewarding experiences, it is easier to be emotionally resilient.

If, however, we continue to delude ourselves that we can control how we feel we will be taken off guard over and over again, meaning we lose the strength to face life when feelings are raw and painful. It is true that, with a committed mindfulness practice, we are going to enhance the quality of our lives; however, no one is immune from emotional pain. We might not be able to control how we feel; nevertheless, we can control how we respond to these feelings.

Exercises

Task 1

Persist with your mindfulness meditation practice every morning for seven days. Watch the life breath and whenever the mental chatter starts to contaminate your practice, come back to the present moment. *You may choose to listen to the guided meditations on the MP3 that was included with this course.*

Task 2

Throughout your day for the next seven days, whenever you are in a bad mood, are fearful of a negative outcome, worrying about a misjudgement or are feeling emotionally heavy and drained, start a new habit of pausing for several minutes and paying complete attention to your breathing. If it helps to take several deep breaths, proceed. Then reflect on someone you love and care about and let that emotion give you a sense of belongingness, support and safety. This simple practice will counteract trying emotions.

Know that perseverance and an ability to flow with the ups and downs are part of hardwiring emotional resilience, which increase your chances of maximising your potential to succeed and prosper.

Task 3

Before you retire at night, for the next seven days, take a self-inventory and monitor your emotional resilience or lack of it. Answer the following questions:

What has your emotional state been like today? Have you been able to persist with your targets and objectives, irrespective of feeling disheartened, hurt or angry? Have you behaved in a professional way? Did you procrastinate on objectives today due to your emotional state? What positive actions did you take today and see through even if you were mentally distracted by other professional, personal or social issues? How did you get on with your 20-minute mindfulness meditation practice this morning? What do you intend to do better tomorrow?

Day 1: Reflect and answer the questions.

Day 2: Reflect and answer the questions.

Day 3: Reflect and answer the questions.

_____

_____
_____
_____
_____
_____
_____
_____
_____
_____
_____
_____
_____
_____
_____
_____
_____
_____
_____
_____
_____
_____
_____
_____
_____
_____
_____
_____
_____
_____

Day 4: Reflect and answer the questions.

Day 5: Reflect and answer the questions.

Day 6: Reflect and answer the questions.

Day 7: Reflect and answer the questions.

A Summary of Week 5

To be emotional resilient – what does this mean?

- To be able to bounce back from upsetting or traumatic experiences
- To respond rationally and calmly to difficulties as they arise
- To be able to calm ourselves down if we find ourselves losing our emotional centre, therefore getting back into the flow of our work
- To be able to handle challenging day-to-day events and still have a sense of emotional wellbeing
- Being flexible in the face of change and being able to tap into our inner reservoir of strength and courage
- Having self-acceptance and a realisation that all things pass
- Train ourselves to be in the present moment

Why is emotional resilience essential in the workplace?

- With emotional resilience hardwired, we are going to find it much easier to practise perseverance.
- Success and effectiveness require emotional resilience to be used as a shield against letting unfriendly emotions get the better of us.
- Emotional resilience helps to sustain emotional wellbeing.
- We cannot truly fulfil our long-term professional goals and objectives without emotional resilience.

Week 6 –
Body Scan Awareness and
Meditation Practices

"Breathe in deeply to bring your mind home to your body."

– Thich Nhat Hanh

Body scan awareness, also referred to as body awareness meditation, is another great mindfulness practice that brings tremendous clarity and peace of mind and has been proven to reduce chronic body pain and release unpleasant physical sensations.

Naturally, we need healthy bodies in order to function. When we bring both mind and body in harmony with one another, we are able to process our emotions, discard unhelpful thoughts and feel centred and serene in the present.

Consider how much stress and toxic emotion is trapped in the bodies of millions of professionals. Over time, this finally takes its toll, with nervous breakdowns and burnout arising. Through practising body scan awareness meditation, we can greatly reduce the detrimental effects of stress and make our working lives pleasant and enjoyable.

Pathological stress in the workplace

Stress disorder has become an increasingly prevalent condition for many in today's workplace and one that is far too often 'hidden' for fear of judgement or lack of understanding.

Stress can be a minimum factor in one's life with a dominant state of calmness, clarity and equanimity. Sadly, all too often the reverse is true. Failure to transcend stress can lead to all sorts of undesirable circumstances and outcomes.

Listed below are the most common triggers which perpetuate pathological stress and its negative effects if not handled with a mindful approach:

- Financial insecurities and concerns about security at work
- Family pressures
- Professional pressures
- A tiresome and rigid routine
- A lack of sufficient downtime
- A lack of sufficient sleep
- Challenging professional relationships
- Unrealistic deadlines

How can too much stress affect our wellbeing?

- Our professional performance will suffer.
- We will be unable to concentrate.
- Our sleeping patterns will be disturbed.

- We will feel unfulfilled, anxious and unhappy.
- Our libido will be affected.
- Professional and personal relationships will be destabilised.
- We will put too much strain on the human heart.

The researcher Holly Utah said in a published statement that: "People who reported higher levels of mindfulness described better control over their emotions and behaviours during the day. In addition, higher mindfulness was associated with lower activation at bedtime, which could have benefits for sleep quality and future ability to manage stress".

Alternate breathing – pranayama

The word 'pranayama', often referred to as alternate breathing, comes from the Sanskrit meaning 'extension of life force' or 'extension of breath'. At times, we are going to have days where we are bombarded with one task after another.

This simple yet effective meditation only takes a couple of minutes and its calming qualities can be felt almost immediately. It is one of the easiest meditation techniques to apply. This practice is well worth applying at least three or four times a day (somewhere private) to develop emotional balance and evenness of mind, especially in the working environment. Below, I have listed instructions for the simplest methods which anyone can enjoy.

How do we apply alternate breathing?

- Close your mouth.
- Press your right index finger over your left nostril.

- Inhale deeply through your right nostril.
- Close your right nostril with your right thumb while keeping your right index finger on your left nostril.
- Pause for several seconds and feel stillness.
- Remove your right index finger from your left nostril and exhale.
- Inhale again through your left nostril (remember that your right thumb is covering your right nostril).
- Pause for several seconds and feel stillness.
- Close your left nostril with your right index finger and remove your right thumb from the right nostril. Exhale through your right nostril.
- Inhale again through your right nostril (while covering your left nostril with your right index finger).
- Continue to alternate this technique for at least three minutes (remembering to pause in between breaths) to gain maximum value.

Mindfully walking and breathing with ease

Many of us have been unconsciously programmed to treat walking as a means to an end, especially while in the workplace. Naturally, a lack of mindfulness while walking leaves one hostage to self-perpetuating stress and anxiety.

We rush (often while shouting into a mobile phone), completely missing the enjoyment of walking. Walking and breathing, if practised harmoniously, can be peaceful and thoroughly enjoyable. Even walking down a corridor or into an office or wherever we are working or being of service can be a harmonious action.

How do we mindfully breathe and walk with ease?

- Bring your attention to your breathing.
- Be aware of how your body naturally glides and has its own rhythm. Notice that our bodies express a natural dance on the earth just as creatures in the sea have a rhythm as they move around the ocean.
- Notice how your muscles move effortlessly.
- Be aware of the feeling of your body being at one with ground thanks to the law of gravity.
- Feel your foot touching and becoming one with the ground.
- Whenever possible, stroll and enjoy walking, remembering that you are breathing.

Breathing and eating mindfully in the workplace

Unless we are mindful and present while eating, we are not really enjoying our food and are likely to squander a much-needed break from work to rest, eat and rejuvenate. Eating mindfully in the workplace demonstrates that you are composed even during your lunch break and will amplify your enjoyment at work.

Shovelling food without any awareness of eating properly usually causes people to eat more than they need, which leaves them feeling bloated and sluggish during the afternoon, meaning that their concentration and energy levels drop. Naturally, this is not conducive to enhancing enthusiasm and outstanding performance. If, however, they are able to be mindful of the entire process of eating they will be able to listen to their stomach and body, informing them that they are full, and resist the tendency to over-eat.

How do we breathe and eat mindfully?

- During the entire process of eating, just as we practise being present in other everyday activities, bring your attention to your breathing.
- Be aware of every movement as you use a knife and fork or perhaps a spoon to cut the food. If you are using your hands to pick up food, notice its texture in your hands.
- Once you have food in your mouth, do not start reaching out to put more food on your fork or spoon or in your hands until you have finished eating what is in your mouth.
- Be aware of the process of chewing your food. Notice the texture and the taste in your mouth and enjoy eating.
- After you have finished chewing, feel the food being swallowed and becoming a part of your body.
- Wait until you have finished swallowing your food before picking up the next mouthful, thus avoiding 'stuffing' your food and over-eating.

'I AM' mindful-breathing technique

'I AM' mindful-breathing is a powerful way to anchor ourselves in inner harmony and peace. When we apply this simple technique into our mindfulness meditation practice, we no longer feel disempowered, separate or lacking in any way. It grounds us into the present moment. As a result, we reduce stress and anxiety. Naturally, we feel abundant and fulfilled.

How do we apply 'I AM' mindful-breathing technique?

- Begin with classic mindfulness meditation, bringing our attention to the life breath and the inner body.
- Notice that we are naturally inhaling and exhaling. As we inhale through our nostrils, silently declare the word 'I'. Make sure the word being expressed lasts as long as you naturally inhale. Then, before you exhale, pause and enjoy a space of stillness.
- After a space of stillness, exhale and silently declare the word 'am'. Make sure the word being expressed lasts as long as you naturally exhale.
- Anytime you drift off into images in the mind, anchor yourself into the present moment through the life breath. Express the words 'I am' with calmness-intensity as you inhale and exhale.
- Apply this meditation for at least 15 minutes. This will gradually (or suddenly) release many artificial collective limitations and restrictions in your mind, thus freeing you to be yourself.

Exercises

Task 1

Persevere with your mindfulness meditation practice every morning for seven days. This time, spend 10 minutes watching the life breath as usual and then for the following 10 minutes, use the following body scan awareness meditation guide. The written guide has been taken from the book, *Mindfulness Meditation: Bringing Mindfulness into Everyday Life*, Chapter 3: Being Present. Spend no more than 30 to

40 seconds on each section outlined as you scan the body. It is very likely that you will feel a tingling sensation as you mindfully scan the body from top to bottom. The sensations will pass and calmness will follow. Persist but do not force—flow with the meditation. ***You may choose to listen to the guided meditations on the MP3 that was included with this course.***

Body awareness meditation guide

a) Bring your attention to the top of your head (to the crown chakra). Be aware of any feelings at the top of your head and keep your attention there for a minute or so.
b) Now bring your attention to your forehead.
c) Now be aware of your eyes, then your nose and ears.
d) Notice any subtle feelings on your cheeks, jaw and face.
e) Be aware of your neck and throat.
f) Then bring your attention to your shoulders.
g) Be aware of your arms and then your hands.
h) Allow yourself to feel your hands then allow energy to flow right to the top of your finger nails and keep your attention there for a minute or so.
i) Now bring your attention to the front of your body and notice your chest.
j) Notice your lungs and then pay attention to your heartbeat.
k) Now be aware of your stomach rising up and down (notice how when you inhale your stomach rises and when you exhale your stomach contracts).
l) Now bring your attention to the back of your body from the back of your head to your spine and do exactly as you did with the front of your body going from top to bottom.
m) Be aware of your back, then your waist and hips down to your thighs, knees, calves and shins, right down to your feet and toes.

Task 2

During your breaks at work, practise a mini body scan awareness meditation or an 'I AM' mindful-breathing technique. For instance, you might just bring your full attention to a particular area in the body. While doing this, use your present moment anchor: the life breath. Being conscious of breathing, eating and walking with awareness and attention.

Task 3

Before you retire at night, for the next seven days, practise body awareness meditation just before you fall asleep. When lying down, feel your chest moving up and down and visually scan your body until you fall asleep. If you follow Week 6's suggestions of meditating in this way as often as possible, stress levels will diminish and tranquillity will be enhanced.

A Summary of Week 6

Mindfulness body scan meditation – what does this mean?

- Being able to process and feel our emotions as we scan the human body from head to toe
- Bringing mind and body into harmony through awareness and attention of the inner body

Alternate breathing – what does this mean?

- Deliberately controlling the flow of the breath through the use of our hands and nostrils
- Being able to alternate the flow of the breath

Mindful breathing, eating and walking – what does this mean?

- We are in tune with the movement of our body as we walk—an anchor into presence.
- We can enjoy eating our food, every mouthful, without the mind creating a sense of hurrying and rushing.
- We can use the breath to remind us to walk and eat mindfully and improve the quality of our lives.

Why are these meditation practices essential in the workplace?

- They amplify our mindfulness practice and enhance calmness and mental stillness.
- They reduce stress and make our lives much easier to emotionally cope with.
- They will play an important part in reducing the risk of professional burnout.
- They will reduce feelings of sluggishness and boost energy levels, particularly in the latter part of the working day.

Week 7 – Self-Compassion

"You cannot serve from an empty vessel."

– Eleanor Brownn

Accept your humanness and the reality that we all make mistakes and have a self-critical dialogue in our mind. Once you fully accept this, the next time you are having a difficult moment you can take a step back and not be too hard on yourself. In other words, if a vicissitude needs to be addressed promptly, proceed but avoid emotional self-harm by beating yourself up with self-recrimination.

First and foremost, if we maintain healthy emotional boundaries and direct love and kindness inwards, we are taking care of ourselves and secondly we are giving a subliminal message to others about how we wish to be treated. People tend to subconsciously treat us how we treat ourselves.

There are many ways to practise self-kindness and this can be a fun and adventurous way of looking after ourselves, even if it is as simple as remembering to sincerely congratulate ourselves after accomplishing an objective.

Plenty of amazing professionals are kind people. Sadly, however, it is staggering how many of them fail to demonstrate kindness to themselves, thus neglecting their own wellbeing. They are kind to their co-workers, bosses, employees, friends and family members, but ask them what sincere kind acts they have done for themselves and many cannot answer the question without floundering. They then wonder why they are often stressed and suffering inside.

To be self-compassionate is not to be self-indulgent or self-centred. A major component of self-compassion is to be kind to yourself. Treat yourself with love, care, dignity and make your wellbeing a priority. With self-compassion, we still hold ourselves accountable professionally and personally, but there are no toxic emotions inflicted upon and towards ourselves.

We can still be assertive, driven and disciplined, as well as being kind and thoughtful. In fact, it would be something of a concern if a driven employer or employee lacked these qualities. Kindness in the workplace reminds us that we are connected to other human beings.

Being kind to yourself and others, on a daily basis, will gradually create an all-round happy working environment. Kindness develops character and helps the person manifesting a kind act to feel better (most of the time), which subsequently elevates mental and emotional wellbeing. It is also a pleasant experience for the person on the receiving end.

Loving-kindness practice in the workplace

Practising loving-kindness (compassionate meditation) in a group several times a week will work wonders by rejuvenating collective harmony and promoting a spirit of cooperation, helping those practising this to transcend stressful and negative emotions. This will also help to engender a spirit of unity amongst employees and help to eliminate any feelings of antagonism.

Loving-kindness, also known as 'metta', is a simple meditation practice that complements the traditional approach to mindfulness and has been proven to bring about outstanding results. The purpose of this practice is to enhance empathy, self-compassion, mental and emotional wellbeing and resilience.

Dr Richard Davidson, a professor of psychology and psychiatry who has been studying compassion and its effect on the human brain, states: "Resilience is the maintenance of high levels of positive affect and wellbeing in the face of adversity. It is not that resilient individuals never experience negative affect, but rather that the negative affect does not persist".

Similarly, the 14th Dalai Lama said: "Compassion really brings about inner peace and inner strength. Those who practise compassion become calmer and less subject to fear".

How to boost success through loving-kindness

I have included a basic guide below for a classic loving-kindness meditation practice.

- First of all, sit down, close your eyes and direct the energy of kindness, compassion, love, peace and prosperity towards yourself.

- Then focus on someone you love or a group of people you cherish. Let this feeling completely bathe your mind, body and heart with the realisation of love and visualise your loved ones enjoying themselves. Wish them love, kindness, peace and prosperity. Deeply realise this feeling for a minute or two.
- Now wish the same for everyone in the same room building as you. Wish them love, kindness, peace and prosperity. Amplify this feeling for a minute or two.
- Focus on someone who disturbs your peace of mind and wish them well, for the sake of releasing any toxic emotions from your mind and body.
- Now bring loving-kindness energy to the planet. Mentally visualise our world and wish for global wellbeing.
- Finally, finish this meditation by considering one thing or person that you are deeply grateful for. After a minute or so, open your eyes.

If you have followed the guide above, you will notice a shift in the way you are feeling towards those around you. This is a powerful practice that will eliminate any bad feeling towards those around you. Naturally, the more you practise loving-kindness, the more you will feel its effects.

If you feel a little bit self-conscious or silly at first while practising this, remind yourself that the facts are that loving-kindness enhances mental and emotional wellbeing.

Exercises

Task 1

Continue with your mindfulness meditation practice every morning but for Week 7 watch your thoughts and emotions and remember to notice that you are breathing for 15 minutes, rather than 20 minutes. *You may choose to listen to the guided meditations on the MP3 that was included with this course.*
Then after 15 minutes of calming the mind, put another five minutes aside to practise a gentle self-compassion meditation by focusing on the following realisations:

- Suffering is a human condition—it is not personal and, therefore, my own suffering is not personal.
- We all suffer and feel pain; therefore, I am not alone. I am accompanied by billions of people on the planet today who also suffer.
- Just because I feel terrible or despondent within myself, that does not mean that I am a terrible person or that I have an awful life, even if I may have acted in ways that are regrettable. If we are fortunate enough to have the insight to use our misfortunes as a springboard to become effective servants in the workplace, then we are truly utilising the good that lies in all human beings. As the aforementioned mindfulness teacher Thich Nhat Hahn pointed out: "Lotus flowers are born in the mud, not on pristine marble".
- My suffering will pass and I can accept that it is there, meaning that I am not at its mercy—I am fully aware and, therefore, I am empowered by my awareness.
  I have the capacity to be kind to myself, to look after myself, to not take my self-criticism as the final word. I have started

right now to honour my wellbeing first and therefore, be a better employer or employee, friend, family member, spouse or partner.

- May I develop a balanced and grounded desire to like myself a little bit more every day and gradually forgive myself for the things I have done in the past that can disturb my peace of mind.

- *Try not to attach a story to the uncomfortable emotions you are experiencing and let go of the temptation to make it into a tragic 'movie' in your mind.*

Task 2

Every day, perform at least one act of kindness towards yourself and another person. Then, reflect in the evenings and make a note of at least one kind thing you have granted yourself and someone else.

Task 3

The final task for Week 7 is to perform at least one act of kindness towards another human being without being credited for it. In other words, do something kind for someone else without being found out. This is a very creative and fun way to be thoughtful and kind and develops a gradual habit of humility and composure.

It might be worth keeping a self-compassionate journal, just as you might have a gratitude journal, just to keep momentum up after the eight-week course has finished.

Day 1: Write down a kind act that you have granted yourself and a kind act that you have carried out for someone else.

_____
_____
_____
_____
_____
_____
_____
_____
_____
_____
_____
_____
_____
_____
_____
_____
_____
_____
_____
_____
_____
_____
_____
_____
_____
_____
_____
_____
_____

Day 2: Write down a kind act that you have granted yourself and a kind act that you have carried out for someone else.

_____

_____

_____

_____

_____

_____

_____

_____

_____

_____

_____

_____

_____

_____

_____

_____

_____

_____

_____

_____

_____

_____

_____

_____

_____

_____

_____

_____

_____

_____

Day 3: Write down a kind act that you have granted yourself and a kind act that you have carried out for someone else.

_____

_____

_____

_____

_____

_____

_____

_____

_____

_____

_____

_____

_____

_____

_____

_____

_____

_____

_____

_____

_____

_____

_____

_____

_____

_____

_____

_____

_____

Day 4: Write down a kind act that you have granted yourself and a kind act that you have carried out for someone else.

_____

_____

_____

_____

_____

_____

_____

_____

_____

_____

_____

_____

_____

_____

_____

_____

_____

_____

_____

_____

_____

_____

_____

_____

_____

_____

_____

_____

Day 5: Write down a kind act that you have granted yourself and a kind act that you have carried out for someone else.

Day 6: Write down a kind act that you have granted yourself and a kind act that you have carried out for someone else.

_____

_____

_____

_____

_____

_____

_____

_____

_____

_____

_____

_____

_____

_____

_____

_____

_____

_____

_____

_____

_____

_____

_____

_____

_____

_____

_____

_____

_____

_____

Day 7: Write down a kind act that you have granted yourself and a kind act that you have carried out for someone else.

_____

_____

_____

_____

_____

_____

_____

_____

_____

_____

_____

_____

_____

_____

_____

_____

_____

_____

_____

_____

_____

_____

_____

_____

_____

_____

_____

_____

A Summary of Week 7

To be self-compassionate – what does this mean?

- Self-compassion is fully accepting our humanness and being able to transcend our negative addictive patterns of behaviour.
- Self-compassion is directing kindness inwards and learning to truly take care of ourselves.
- Self-compassion is a realisation of feeling connected to humanity, rather than feeling isolated.
- Self-compassion is to be mindful of our own needs and be true to ourselves in any given situation.
- Self-compassion is to bring comfort and understanding to ourselves.
- Self-compassion is to start a life-long process of self-acceptance and self-forgiveness.

Why is self-compassion important?

- We are far more likely to burnout and suffer from stress if we lack a practice of self-compassion.
- It helps us to look after our mental, emotional and physical wellbeing.
- We know when to pause and have a higher awareness of reality and can thus communicate better and become more effective in our work and personal lives.
- It's easier to be successful if we honour our wellbeing.
- We are no longer dominated by ill feeling towards ourselves or others.

Week 8 – Cultivating Gratitude and Appreciation in the Workplace

"Gratitude turns what we have into enough, and more. It turns denial into acceptance, chaos into order, confusion into clarity... it makes sense of our past, brings peace for today, and creates a vision for tomorrow."

— Melody Beattie

Like gratitude, authentic appreciation in the workplace is a realisation that can be nurtured and accessed with daily mindful practice. By and large, people who are grateful, happy and enthusiastic are going to demonstrate better performance than those who are unhappy and unappreciative. There is increasing evidence that a grateful mindset amplifies happiness and mental and emotional wellbeing.

More often than not, we decide well in advance what will make us appreciative or unappreciative. We have more power than we realise to develop the habit of gratitude and happiness in our professional and personal lives. There are several daily exercises outlined below, which will assist you to enhance a subtle authentic happiness in your day-to-day life.

The happiest man in the world

The French interpreter for the 14th Dalai Lama, former academic and dedicated meditator Matthieu Ricard, came into the spotlight in the field of neural science after being named "the happiest man in the world".

Naturally, there are many other men and women who demonstrate such equanimity, but the studies on his brain uncovered truly astonishing results. MRI scans showed that Matthieu Ricard and other serious long-term meditators (with more than 10,000 hours of practice each) were mentally, emotionally and spiritually fulfilled and displayed an abundance of positive emotions and equanimity in the left pre-frontal cortex of the brain.

When talking about his mindfulness training, Matthieu Ricard said with humility that: "Happiness is a skill. It requires effort and time".

Gratitude and conscious breathing cleanse the human mind

Most of us understand the necessity of keeping ourselves clean by having a daily bath or shower. Many of us have also become conscious of the importance of eating healthily. Naturally, we feel much better after a shower or after eating a healthy meal. Similarly, it's important to cleanse our minds through conscious breathing.

During a long day of challenges at work, with thoughts of failure and emotions of frustration, a moment of remembering and appreciating that our breathing works wonders. Therefore, let us respect and appreciate our breathing.

Just as we realise that it is essential to pause throughout the day and breathe properly, it is also important to smile—not a fake, insincere smile, but a genuine one. This simple act affects our mood and can create a sense of unity, gratitude and friendliness amongst staff, clients, family and the general public.

This is what the American writer William Arthur Ward meant by "A warm smile is the universal language of kindness". If we pay attention to life, we notice that we have many reasons to smile. We communicate far better with people when we are appreciative and grateful for what we have, for our life and for the opportunity to be of service.

A thankful attitude makes us feel centred, grounded and calm. Even when a situation at work irritates or unsettles us, an appreciation for what we have can make all the difference. When we remember how incredible it is to be breathing or simply to be alive in the here and now, pleasant feelings will follow.

Through conscious mindful breathing, we realise how wonderful it is to have loved ones and friends, to be living on planet Earth and for the inspiring activities that manifest all over the world—we feel grateful and satisfied with the present.

When we can appreciate the qualities of another human being, the sweet scent of a flower or the taste of a delicious meal, we feel abundant and enriched. Naturally, this awareness in the workplace will eradicate undesirable negative emotions and produce a collective mental uplift.

When we flow and are in tune with the life breath, we are far more equipped to deal with challenges as they arise in the present. Therefore, let us flow with the ups and downs and remain steady, resilient, mindful and calm and, of course, remember to breathe deeply and gently.

Gratitude reduces the fear of financial insecurity

Fear engendered by the feeling of financial insecurity is a deep-rooted and universal human condition. The fear of financial insecurity is ultimately a fear of drawing closer to death.

This debilitating fear, if not tempered on a daily basis, can trigger anxiety, panic attacks, anger, resentment, self-pity, jealousy and even depression. It can lead to irrational and illogical behaviour, even for the calmest of us. By and large, this fear comes and goes but lies dormant in most of us.

Anxiety caused by financial insecurity can be tempered by discussing concerns in a supportive environment or with a spouse/partner, friend or family member who is understanding; however, the most effective way to transcend this fear is by cultivating gratitude. It is through expressing gratitude that we remind ourselves just how fortunate we are to have what we have. When we fear losing our source (or sources) of income, the emotional state we are displaying is that we are lacking and do not have enough, which clouds our perspective and can distort reality.

Ideally, writing in a regular gratitude journal soothes these insecurities. For instance, how can we feel that we are/will be lacking in our lives when we remember who we love and that we are loved? When we make a note of the people, places and things we appreciate, we change our perspective. A sense of gratitude is something that has to be cultivated and worked on. Sometimes, we feel spontaneously grateful, but most of the time a feeling of thankfulness has to be engendered by our efforts.

Sharing gratitude with a group of friends or co-workers on a daily basis will induce a positive, cheerful and abundant atmosphere in the workplace.

For example, when we feel flat or despondent, we can remind ourselves how fortunate we are to be in employment and to be lucky enough to contribute to society. We can remember to appreciate our mental faculties, which permit us to serve and be effective. We can even go deeper and appreciate the hardships in life that have forced us to evolve and consequently become the person we are today. The list is endless.

Exercises

Task 1

Continue with your mindfulness meditation practice every morning for a full seven-day week, putting a minimum of 20 minutes aside to observe the natural flow of your breathing and watch your thoughts and emotions. *You may choose to listen to the guided meditations on the MP3 that was included with this course.*

Task 2

Whenever you start to feel disconnected from yourself, take a five-minute break and come back to your breathing; subsequently, ponder something or someone who makes you laugh and then allow yourself to laugh. If it helps, go for a walk and call a friend or talk to a trusted co-worker and focus on comedy. This will assist you to release stress, strain and tension in the body. This mini practice only takes five minutes and will reboot your energy and happiness.

Another mental tool to enhance gratitude is to make a conscious effort to focus on those you love and those who love you. Focus on people who inspire you and flow into thankfulness for them. Neuropsychologist and writer Dr Rick Hanson suggests that if we create a positive emotion, such as gratitude, and hold onto this feeling for 10 seconds (no less), the brain starts to rewire itself. The key is to do this several times a day and bathe the brain with appreciation.

Task 3

Every evening before retiring, write a gratitude list of 20 things that you appreciated in the day. Even if it is a subtle appreciation for something like being able to have a shower or a bath or a delicious meal, a friendly conversation with a client or colleague, or a smile from a stranger, write it down.

Day 1: What can you be grateful for, regardless of whether you have had a good or bad day?

_____

_____

_____

_____

_____

_____

_____

_____

_____

_____

_____

_____

_____

_____

_____

_____

_____

_____

_____

_____

_____

_____

_____

_____

_____

_____

_____

_____

Day 2: What are you grateful for with respect to today's activities?

Day 3: What can you appreciate about today?

Day 4: Write down 10 things, in general, that you are thankful for.

_____
_____
_____
_____
_____
_____
_____
_____
_____
_____
_____
_____
_____
_____
_____
_____
_____
_____
_____
_____
_____
_____
_____
_____
_____
_____
_____
_____
_____

Day 5: Write down 10 things that you appreciate about your work,
your clients, members of staff and the general feeling at work.

Day 6: Write down 10 things that you appreciate about your family, friends and loved ones.

Day 7: Write down 10 things that you appreciate about your talents, skills and finer qualities.

A Summary of Week 8

To be grateful and appreciative – what does this mean?

- To feel emotionally grounded and thankful for the present moment
- To be in an emotional state of abundance and plenty, instead of operating from a mindset of scarcity and neediness
- To feel connected to your heart, mind and body
- A sense of joy to be alive and breathing
- To have a realisation of self-acceptance and peace of mind

Why is gratitude and appreciation essential in the workplace?

- Gratitude and appreciation enhance mental and emotional wellbeing.
- It puts challenges at work into perspective and helps to shape a positive frame of mind.
- It sparks enthusiasm and energy in the workplace.
- It anchors us into the nowness of life and keeps us centred and at ease with challenges at work.
- It plays a major role in reducing the risk of pathological stress and burnout.
- It reduces negative self-talk and ill feeling.
- Gratitude can increase authentic happiness.

Afterword

Afterword
A Modern Mindful Workplace

"Mindfulness of oneself cultivates wisdom. Mindfulness of others
cultivates compassion."

— Stonepeace

As I write this Epilogue, scientific papers are being released every
week with new evidence demonstrating that mindfulness is an
exceptional tool that can amplify the wellbeing of humanity. It has
taken over 2,600 years for both the East and West to seriously
appreciate what mindfulness and calmness can do to make the world,
and, of course, the workplace, a better place.

From the modest pockets of the men and women scattered around
the world who sat for hours at a time in silence and reflection, to
modern-day scientists, doctors and professors, meditation is
becoming widely accepted as a logical and rational practice that can
enhance our lives.

I am thrilled to see that the West has become more open to the
ancient Wisdom Traditions, from studying the mental techniques to
testing them out in our most prestigious universities; mindfulness

meditation is becoming hardwired into our collective mental and emotional language.

Granted, mindfulness will not solve all of our problems; nonetheless, it can address many of our mental, emotional and physical challenges. One thing we know is that the more awareness we have, the more power we have to learn new things, discover and uncover nature's great secrets and accomplish breakthroughs to address disease and poverty.

More companies large and small are adopting mindfulness practices, including yoga breathing techniques; this inspires me deeply. The Bank of England has run mindfulness pilot sessions and companies like Google and Transport for London (TFL) have embraced the practice. It is comforting to know that more businesses are recognising the importance of mental and emotional wellbeing in the workplace.

It is my deepest hope that you have gained value from this book. Whether you have gained value from the entire text, the exercises or an idea that personally made sense to you, then my intention has been fulfilled.

Life is challenging and the workplace can bring us both joy and sorrow. The moments of triumph and the moments of hardship, however, are what can make our professional lives vibrant, fresh and creative. Let us never forget how lucky we are to be able to work and contribute to society in this day and age.

Appendix

Appendix I – Burnout

The English Oxford Dictionary describes 'burnout' as "Physical or mental collapse caused by overwork or stress". Essentially, burnout is a psychological term that refers to long-term exhaustion and apathy for one's professional, social and even personal life. Full-blown burnout is a complete lack of interest in life, which can lead to other serious mental complications.

Burnout occurs when we feel overwhelmed and utterly pressured to meet both professional and personal demands. The person begins to lose motivation in their profession. Many people live within the periphery of burnout and are suffering mentally and emotionally.

Burnout is increasingly common in the public sector: medical doctors, social workers, psychiatric nurses, therapists and substance misuse workers are all subject to intolerable levels of stress and frustration, which often culminate in complete physical, mental and emotional breakdown. Burnout is also rife in the private sector, affecting many bankers, lawyers and accountants.

The psychological term known as 'burnout' was coined by Herbert Freudenberger, the German-born American psychologist, in his book *Staff Burnout*, which was published in 1974. According to Freudenberger, there are 12 phases that lead to burnout:

1.   The Compulsion to Prove Oneself
2.   Working Harder
3.   Neglecting Their Needs
4.   Displacement of Conflicts
5.   Revision of Values
6.   Denial of Emerging Problems
7.   Withdrawal
8.   Obvious Behavioral Changes
9.   Depersonalisation
10.   Inner Emptiness
11.   Depression
12.   Burnout Syndrome

Professional burnout has become a grave concern for many businesses and governments due to the enormous financial cost that comes with it. Professional burnout affects people from all walks of life and does not discriminate.

Burnout is characterised by disengagement, whereas someone who is stressed will be more likely to show signs of over-engagement. Professionals who are overly stressed are still able to function and subconsciously feel that if they can only 'manage' things better, they will be 'better'.

A professional who has burnout, however, feels that nothing they do will make things 'better'. They are completely isolated mentally and emotionally from their external environment and their own needs. They feel utterly hopeless and despair is a common trait in their mindset.

Appendix II – Presence and present

The English Oxford Dictionary describes presence as "The state or fact of existing, occurring, or being present", "A person or thing that exists or is present in a place but is not seen" or "The impressive manner or appearance of a person".

Presence in the meditation field means bringing our entire 'being' (as in our heart, mind, body and consciousness) into the present moment, fully and without compromise. Presence is being emotionally present and available and bringing the awareness of our internal reality into the 'here and now'.

The poet Rumi, for example, gave us a brilliant description of the simplicity of presence in the book *The Essential Rumi*: "Your hand opens and closes, opens and closes. If it were always a fist or always stretched open, you would be paralysed. Your deepest presence is in every small breath contracting and expanding, the two as beautifully balanced and coordinated as birds' wings".

Appendix III – Stillness

Stillness in the mindfulness or meditation field is not necessarily being physically still or without movement. Rather, it is an inner silence and a calmness in the human mind. The word 'stillness' is frequently used in yoga teachings and meditation literature.

Stillness is essentially a gap between our thoughts. These gaps can last for a second or two and can sometimes last up to several minutes or even several hours. The gaps or 'spaces' are very difficult to describe in words, but they are essentially a feeling of pure bliss, joy, peace and content without prolonged thought activity or mental self-talk.

For instance, if you observe your mental activity, there is a constant stream of thoughts (images, pictures, etc.), emotions and mental chatter. The stream seldom stops but for the occasional space, which comes as a sigh of relief.

For example, a clock ticks every second but between the ticking is a minute space of silence. Now, let us pretend that every second represents a 'thought' and the tiny gap represents 'no thought'. The 'no thought' is 'stillness'.

During this reprieve from compulsive thinking, everything we observe looks bright, shiny and brand new, as though we were 'seeing' for the first time, just as we did as babies and very young infants. Thoughts give objects labels. Transcend the thought, however, and there is no mental commentary. Instead, there is just a pure awareness of the object—a stillness.

Stillness cannot be forced but we can experience it on a regular basis through daily mindfulness practices and meditation techniques. Quite often, stillness comes to us when we least expect it and can last for several minutes at a time.

Appendix IV – Wisdom Traditions

The Wisdom Traditions are essentially a transcendental approach to mystic spiritual realisations that can be found in the wise ancient texts and spiritual writings that are free from sectarianism, doctrinal literalism and political power structures. In most religious texts, universal gems of wisdom can be found which cross over to all aspects of human life.

The Wisdom Traditions provide an internal framework for a spiritual life which realises enlightenment and inner fulfilment.

These different Wisdom Traditions are often practised by applying yoga or meditation, studying classic transcendental literature, listening to music and chanting mystical mantras. Many practices such as yoga and mindfulness, which stem from the Wisdom Traditions (such as Zen/Buddhism), have become mainstream in the 21st Century due to the scientific evidence of yoga and meditation being an essential ingredient in mental, emotional and physical health and wellbeing.

Appendix V – Meditation

According to the English Cambridge Dictionary, the word 'meditation' is described as: "The act of giving your attention to only one thing, either as a religious activity or as a way of becoming calm and relaxed" or "Serious thought or study, or the product of this activity".

Because there is such an abundance of approaches to meditation, however, it is almost impossible to give a clear-cut direct description of what meditation actually is, just as there are various debates about what it means to be 'intelligent'.

In almost every religion or spiritual text, the word meditation is used. Naturally, this can create all sorts of negative connotations, ambivalence and discrimination. For instance, some people believe that thinking about their past in a reflective tone is a meditation. Others would exclaim that life in itself is a meditation. Still others would suggest that meditation is observing your thoughts and emotions and inner body. Many also point out that every time we are conscious of our breathing (every conscious breath) is a meditation. His Holiness, the 14th Dalai Lama, once said "sleep is the best meditation".

Mindfulness meditation is a practice that has been around for over 2,600 years and first developed in the East. The meditation practice of observing awareness of awareness and thought/emotion came from the early Buddhist and Zen movement.

Many meditation practices have been carefully designed to create authentic happiness, compassion, bliss, empathy, understanding, forgiveness and generosity. Some practices are more science-based, attempting to understand consciousness, the nature of consciousness and the awareness of consciousness.

In the 21st Century, the word 'meditation' is being used far more frequently in the scientific and medical fields than ever before.

Appendix VI – Anxiety

According to the UK National Health Service: "Anxiety is a feeling of unease, such as worry or fear, that can be mild or severe".

We can all feel anxious for different reasons. People might feel anxious because they are nervous about an outcome or because they are trying something for the first time or are just about to undergo an operation. This is not abnormal and is a universal human condition.

Unfortunately, many people find it extremely difficult to transcend their worries and feel anxious most of the time. This is often described as 'low-level anxiety' and can be a general feeling of 'dis-ease' or emotional discomfort. More extreme types of anxiety include social anxiety disorder, panic disorder, post-traumatic stress disorder and phobias, all of which can be severely incapacitating.

The practice of mindfulness has been proven to greatly reduce anxiety and most anxiety disorders.

Appendix VII – Zen

Zen is a school of Mahayana Buddhism that came to fruition in China during the Tang dynasty, which became a popular practice in Japan and is now an internally recognised meditation practice.

The legend of Zen is that the Buddha was sitting amongst his early followers, who wanted to fully understand enlightenment and the practice of mindfulness meditation. The Buddha picked up a flower and held it up, observing it for several minutes without saying a single word. He then put it down, stood up and walked away, leaving most of his followers confused and bewildered.

However, a handful of the men understood what the Buddha had done, which was to observe the flower without mentally labelling it. The men who understood taught this meditation to pockets of people, which gradually caused the flowering of the Zen movement.

Unlike many meditation schools and sects in Buddhism that focus on knowledge, information and religious doctrine, Zen is geared towards the personal understanding and realisation of an internal reality and the present moment. This practice is usually practised with a Zen teacher through Zazen meditation.

Zazen literally means "seated meditation", during which a Zen student or master will sit on a cushion in a lotus position and fold their hands in the cosmic mudra. This is accomplished by placing the dominant hand palm upward, while holding the other hand also faced palm up. The thumbs are lightly touching.

The practice generally focuses on observing the life breath and letting emotions, feelings and thoughts come and go as they please without trying to control or manipulate them. Zazen also encourages students to watch and count the breath flow in and out of the body to bring about a realisation of stillness and tranquillity.

Zen and Zazen essentially bring awareness to the present moment as it is and integrate mind and body—Zen is a way of being, rather than a philosophy.

A Thank-You Note From the Author

Dear Reader,

I hope you have gained value from the course and participated in the exercises to gain maximum fulfilment. I would like to thank you for being open-minded enough to read, study and apply yourself to this book.

Although this book is outlined as an 8-week course, if you have followed it through to the final week, you'll probably get a sense that mindfulness is a full-time practice and will bring great benefit to you, helping you to continue applying yourself to present-moment awareness and a mindful life.

You're more than welcome to send me an email to let me know how you got on with the course.

If you have any comments or would like to know more about MBP, email me at christopher@christopherdines.com

I wish you peace of mind and success,

Christopher Dines

www.mindfulnessburnoutprevention.org
www.christopherdines.com

Acknowledgements

Thank you so much to La Petite Fleur Publishing for taking a risk and publishing this book and for your belief in my work over the years. Thank you to Mary McGahan for editing the book and for your encouragement and support. Thank you so much to Dr Barbara Marisposa for writing the foreword.

Thank you to Laura Gordon for designing the book cover and for your positive artistry over the last two years that have contributed to my work. Thank you to Lizzie Ferrar for proofreading my work and for a professional attitude. Thank you to marketing designer Danny Kent, in Spain, for your efficient and excellent work.

Thank you to Mr James Alexander for your time, encouragement and sharing your wisdom. Thank you to Lester Morse for your continued encouragement and generosity.

A special thank you to Mum and Dad, family, friends and to everyone serving in the mindfulness/self-awareness field who is making a positive contribution to the United Kingdom and the world.

About the Author

I essentially train people to access the present moment through mindfulness, which is the gateway to equanimity, clarity and calmness.

This is particularly effective during a group meditation. With gentle persistent practice, they are able to separate their thoughts and emotions from themselves rather than being swept away by negative self-talk—they have accessed self-awareness and emotional intelligence. This training has been scientifically proven to greatly reduce addictive thinking, stress, strain and burnout. It has also been demonstrated to be wonderfully effective in the treatment of addiction, anxiety and depression.

Biography

Christopher Francis Dines (born 19th August 1983) is an English mindfulness teacher, trainer, writer and founder of Mindfulness Burnout Prevention (MBP).

Having a deep love for music, Christopher left high-school at 15 to pursue a full-time career as an electronic house DJ. Having DJ'ed at prestigious venues such as City Loud at Turnmills, Ministry of Sound, Defected In The House at Pacha and Garage City, Christopher's DJ'ing career took him to Asia where he travelled extensively. This subsequently led him to remix and produce underground electronic dance music.

While remixing national chart hit band Afro Medusa to artists such Marlon D, Samba La Casa, Steal Vybe and Onxy (Soul2Soul), mindfulness was gradually becoming a subtle practice. This led to a deep exploration of the human mind and roads to emotional wellbeing and self-realisation. This has been accomplished through intense self-education and with the invaluable help and guidance of enlightened mentors.

He 'retired' from the electronic dance music industry in June 2006 to give public talks on inspirational ideas and self-awareness and create personal development and mindfulness workshops and courses. Christopher Dines trains employers, employees and self-referrals to amplify emotional intelligence, emotional resilience and mindfulness in the workplace.

Christopher is the author of *Mindfulness Meditation: Bringing Mindfulness into Everyday Life, Manifest Your Bliss: A Spiritual Guide to Inner Peace, A Ticket to Prosperity, A Ticket to Prosperity: Spiritual Lessons for an Abundant Life* (Revised Edition), *The Mystery of Belief: How to Manifest Your Dreams, and Mindfulness Burnout Prevention: An 8-Week Course for Professionals.*